Words Defined Prophetically

"A Dictionary for Revelational Minds"

Robert L. Robinson Th.D

Words Defined Prophetically

To Mom, be blessed, thanks for your many words of encouragement

Preface

Words Defined Prophetically

"The Dictionary for Revelational Minds"

  Words Defined Prophetically is a book containing a selection of Biblical, Hebrew and Greek words detailing information concerning their meaning. It serves as a dictionary to those who are new believers, students of scripture or seasoned believers. These words are those used in our everyday language within the Christian community and in ministry as a whole. In many situations believers have sat and listened to the Word of God going forth and would hear certain words or terms coming forth out of the Word and would wonder of their meanings. This dictionary assists in answering some of those questions which may arise while hearing the Word.

  What is meant by the term "Revelational Minds?" Jesus said in Philippians' 2:5 to "Let this mind be in you, which was also in Christ Jesus." He was stating that the believer needed to have the mind of Christ which is a mind of revelation. The word revelation means "the unveiling of truth which is the true intended interpretation of the Spirit." The revelational mind is one that has been born again and sees and understands the true intended interpretation of the scriptures. Another term for revelational minds is "revelation knowledge." Revelational knowledge comes through the Holy Spirit and the believer who desires such must posses the ability to be open and in some situations be changed by what is released.

  This dictionary is a reference tool to those who have sought a reliable source for revelatory and prophetic definitions. It is not however, for the non-believer, nor is it for the carnal minded because the non-believer or the carnal minded will not nor cannot receive the things that are being released in the Spirit. It serves as a tool which causes the believer to have a desire to want to know the Father the more; it will complement those who have Bible knowledge and cause them to pursuit the very heart of God the more.

Table of Contents

Abaddon – the name of the angel of the bottomless pit mentioned in Revelation 9:11. In the Hebrew his name is Abaddon, but in the Greek his name Apollyon. The name means destruction and is an end time ruling spirit.

Abomination – that which is morally disgusting in the presence of the Lord.

Abraham – He was a Chaldean that became the founding patriarch of the Hebrew nation. Abraham was a man of faith and is referred to as "the Father of faith." He was challenged by God to leave his country, family, and from his father's house and go to a place that God would show him. The original name of Abraham was Abram. Both names have the same meaning. The name Abraham is made up of two words ab which means father and raham with means lifted. In the name Abram, Ab means father and ram means lifted. So, both names have the same meaning. Why then would God change the name of Abram to Abraham if both are the same? The reason being is because if a person has authority over something then that individual has the right and responsibility to name it. Abram was named by his father Terah who had authority over Abram. But, when Abram left his father's house, God, who respected the authority of Terah, now took over as being Abrams authority and changed Abrams name to Abraham. The change in the name indicated change in authority. God cut covenant with Abraham and made him a father of many nations and he walked in covenantal authority. One of the most powerful stories among the Hebrews is called the Akedah which is the story of the binding up of his son Isaac. (See Akedah)

Accusation - The word accusation is the Hebrew word sitnah (sit-naw'). The word sitnah comes from the Hebrew word satan (saw-tan') which means, "To attack, accuse, be an adversary, resist." The word accusation is a word of attack from the adversary.

Ahab - The son of Omri, whom he succeeded as the seventh king of Israel. The history of Ahab is recorded in 1 Kings 16-22. Ahab was married to Jezebel and it was the first time that a king of Israel had allied himself by marriage with a heathen princess. Ahab is responsible for the ultimate ruin of Israel. Omri the father of Ahab was noted as the worst king of that time, until Ahab took over the reign. Jezebel was a heathen princess who was responsible for introducing the worship of Baal to Israel. (See Jezebel)

Akedah – one of the most powerful narratives in the Hebrew Bible. It is a Hebrew term that means "binding" and is in reference to Abraham's binding of Isaac upon the altar at Mt. Moriah. One of the reasons for the blowing of the shofar during the Holy Days is that it serves as a reminder of the ram sacrifice in the place of Isaac. The story of the Akedah is recognized as the 10th and climatic test for Abraham.

Aleph - The first letter of the Hebrew alphabet. Aleph is also noted in the word oxen noted in Psalms 144:14. The word oxen in the Hebrew is the word alluph which means a gentle or tamed ox. .

Aliyah – means "going up" and refers to a person chosen to read from the torah in the Jewish synagogue. Being chosen to read from the Torah was considered an honor.

Altar of Incense - The altar of incense was made of shittim wood (incorruptible) and overlaid with gold (purity of Christ). It was 1-½ feet by 1-½ feet by 3 feet. There were four horns made of gold that sat on each corner of the altar. Two rings were placed on each side of the altar and through those two rings went staves of shittim wood overlaid with gold. The altar of incense was placed in the center of the room in the sanctuary in front of the mercy seat (though the veil separated it). The altar of incense represents sacrificial praise. Praise is the second level of one's worship experience. (See incense)

Amen – The word amen means "let the will of the Lord be done as it is proclaimed." When individuals say amen they in essence are saying, " I agree with what has been decreed so let the will of the Lord be done."

Anointing - To anoint" means to consecrate and ordain a person or thing for a particular office, function, or service. In the Old Testament, the word anointing comes from the Hebrew word mishchah, which means "unction (the act)." Its root, mashach, means "to rub with oil, to anoint; by implication, to consecrate; also to paint; smear." The noun form of the Hebrew word mashach is Messiah. The Greek word for anoint is chrio, while the Greek noun is Christos, which means, "to anoint." The word "anoint" then is associated with Messiah or Christ, which implies that one cannot have anointing without The Anointed One (Ps.133: 1-2). Anointing serves as an equipping for service. It calls for submission and alignment to God's order. (See unction)

Apostle – This word is made up of two words the first being apo which means off or away. The second word being stello which means to be set apart with the idea of sending away. The word apostle means to be set apart, sent away or sent. The word apostle was used of men who were naval officers responsible for an entire fleet of ships that were sent away for a specific purpose or objective. The term applies to apostles today who are commissioned by God and sent with a specific objective. Apostles are sent from a place to a place with orders and their objective is to follow through with those orders.

Apostle's of the Lamb – The Apostles of the Lamb were the original twelve who were responsible for establishing the early Church. Their qualifications were that they were eyewitnesses of the earthly ministry of Jesus and had to have witnessed His resurrection. (Acts 1:15-22; Rev. 21:14).

Apostolic – this word is derived from the word apostle which means "one sent from a place to a place with orders." To be apostolic means to function under the anointing of being sent. One is not necessarily an apostle but you do function under an anointing which makes the works that is done apostolic.

Apostolic Succession (prophetically) – Prophetically speaking apostolic succession is the passing down of kingdom authority whereby it allows the work of the kingdoms vision to continue unhindered. Spiritual fathers may pass away (sleep) however the work that the Father had begun in them will not cease because that work along with an anointing would be passed down allowing that work to continue.

Apothecary - one who prepares holy oils and ointments. Priests were properly qualified for this office. Prophetically speaking, an apothecary is a worshipper mainly a worship leader who's anointed to properly place together songs of praise and worship to be offered up before the Lord.

Ark of the Covenant - The Ark of the Covenant was a box 45 inches long and 27 inches wide made of shittim wood (incorruptible wood Ps. 16:10). The Ark was to be covered with gold on the inside and outside. The lid of the Ark was a separate piece called the Mercy-Seat. It was 3 feet 9 inches by 2 feet 3 inches. The lid secured and completed the box. It represents the finished work, the established order, that which was tried, tested, and found true. The lid also reveals the unchanging, unbroken spoken and revealed Word of God. Inside the ark were three articles: a golden pot that had manna, Aaron's rod that budded, and the tables of the covenant (Heb. 9:4). Two cherubs of hammered gold were placed above the mercy-seat. One cherub at one end of the lid and another at the other end, their faces pointed downward towards the mercy seat as they were connected together at their wings which covered the mercy seat. The jobs of the cherubs were to guard the glory and the holiness of the Lord. The Spirit of God would rest between the 2 wings of the cherubs that were above the Mercy-Seat. The Ark of the Covenant was the throne of God and presence of God on earth.

Ark of the Covenant (contents) - There was three articles in the Ark of the Covenant, the two tablets, Manna and Aaron's rod that budded. The 2 tablets were the Law of the book of Covenant and they were placed in the side of the Ark. (Deut. 31:9-26). The tablets prophetically speak of God's divine Word, His precepts, and His commandments. They shadowed forth the Lord Jesus who alone kept the Covenant and Laws of God perfectly for that Law was in His heart (Heb. 10:5-7). The tablets in the Ark of the Covenant denoted the structured unbreakable non-changing unadulterated Word of the Lord. Manna was another of the contents in the Ark of the Covenant. Manna was given to the Children of Israel while they were in the wilderness and it sustained them. Manna denotes the keeping, sustaining power of God's Word; it sustains the believer in their darkest hour. The third article in the Ark of the Covenant was Aaron's rod that budded. The rod was used in order to choose a priest. A rod from each tribe was placed in the tabernacle and the rod that budded denoted that the leader of that particular tribe would be the high priest. Aaron's rod, which represented the tribe of Levi, budded, which meant that Aaron was to be the first high priest and mediator. The budding rod denotes the choosing of the Lord and also the Lord watching over those whom He chooses.

Asaph - One of David's chief musicians whose job was to conduct with cymbals the music performed in the tent where the ark was housed (1 Chron. 16:4-7, 37). Asaph was also a prophet and he was King David's seer. Asaph was a steward over the music ministry and is noted as being the person responsible for writing Psalms chapters fifty and seventy-three through eighty-three.

Asher - the eighth son of Jacob and the father of the tribe of Asher, one of the twelve tribes of Israel. Asher assisted in the plot to sell Joseph into slavery. Jacob on his deathbed prophesied that would come the richest food; he will provide the king's delights.

Ashtoreth - The moon goddess of the Phoenicians who was worshipped as the goddess of nature. To the Zidonians she was the Ishtar or goddess of war. Solomon promoted his wives' idolatry by building temples to Ashtoreth. Josiah defiled these idols and their places of worship on the Mount of Olives by breaking down their images and groves (2 Kings 23:13-14). In Jeremiah 44:25 the goddess Ashtoreth is called the "queen of heaven." It is believed that Athaliah the daughter of Ahab and Jezebel worshipped this goddess. This spirit denotes one of war, prostitution, and licentious worship. (See Zidonians, the)

Athaliah - the daughter of Jezebel who inherited her mother's cruelty and ruthlessness. She married Jehoram, king of Judah, and influenced him and their son Ahaziah to reintroduce Baal worship (a false seed religion). She became Queen Mother of Judah, and it was during this time that she became a barbarian. Athaliah was a vision killer, a murderer who will kill anyone or anything who may pose as a threat to her program. Athaliah was a woman who had to be in control and would never be in subjection to anyone. Athaliah denotes an anointing and seed killer, she represents a destroyer of inheritance, and she hates spiritual authority and Truth.

Atonement (Day of) – The Hebrew expression for the Day of Atonement is Yom Kippur, which means Day of Covering. This day was observed on the tenth day of the seventh month Tishre and is considered the most holiest and solemn day in the Jewish calendar. On this day the priest would enter into the Holy of Holies three times in that one day. The first time, he entered the Holy of Holies with the incense. The second time the priest entered the Holy of Holies with the blood of the bullock, which atoned for his own sins and those in his house. The third time the priest entered the

Holy of Holies with the blood of the goat for the sins of the people (which would produce forgiveness and blessing). Prophetically speaking, the Day of Atonement is a time when the people become one with Christ; it is a time of sacrifice. It will cause us to afflict our souls allowing the proving process of God to take place in our lives. (See Passover, unleavened bread, firstfruits, Pentecost, day of the trumpet, Day of Atonement, feast of Tabernacles).

Ayin - the sixteenth letter of the Hebrew alphabet and is defined as "eye." "Behold, the eye of the Lord is upon them that fear him, upon them that hope in his mercy." (Psalms 33:18) Ayin denotes the ever seeing eye of the Lord being upon His people.

Baal – the chief idol god worshipped by the Canaanites and was referred to as the sun god. The worship of baal involved lewdness, bloody orgies, human sacrifice and ceremonial prostitution and was constantly resorted to by many worshipers of Yahweh because of its high sensual appeal. Baal worship often required male prostitution as their ceremonies consisted of gay licentiousness between the sodomites and the worshippers. Those prostitutes were brought into the worship to serve the priesthood and engulf worshippers with perverse ritualistic sexual acts.

Baasha – king of Israel who was known for his idolatries. God pronounced judgment upon Baasha through the mouth of Jehu the prophet. Baasha's idolatries led to his family being exterminated, according to the word of the prophet Jehu (1 Kings 16:3, 4, 10-13). (See Jehu spirit of)

Balaam – the name means "devourer of the people, devourer or destroyer." He was a prophet of God who was approached by Balak the king of Moabites to curse the Israelites when they were encamped in the Plains of Moab. The king eventually offered Balaam riches and honor that caused Balaam to give in to the advances and in doing so betrayed Israel. Joshua 13:22 refer to Balaam as a soothsayer. Prophetically Balaam speaks of a prophet who completely gave in to the enemy and has become a false prophet for hire whose motivation is silver and gold.

Babel (Tower of) – The tower of Babel (Gen. 10:10) was a tower built by people who attempted to reach heaven. In Genesis 10:10 the bible refers to Babel as the beginning of Nimrod's kingdom. The Greek form of this word means "the gate of god", the Hebrew form of Babel means confusion. Babel denotes mans attempt to reach God in a way in which God has not sanctioned, the outcome of that attempt is becoming confused.

Babylon - The word Babylon is the Hebrew word Babel (baw-bel'), which means "confusion." Its root word means, "An overflowing." Babylon is a place of overflowing confusion.

Badgers (skin) - Badgers skin was a leather-like substance used to cover the tabernacle, the ark, and other sacred objects. The covering also protected the Tabernacle when the children of Israel were in transition. Prophetically the badgers skin denotes the covering and protection through prayer. (See Goats skins, Rams skin)

Baptism (Water) – One of the doctrines of the Church. The baptism in water is the total submersion of a believer into water denoting their identification with the new birth in Christ Jesus. Baptism in water reveals a solid foundation in the life of the believer. The word baptism comes from the Greek word baptize is baptizo (bap-tid'-zo), which means, "to make whelmed or fully wet. (see baptism corporate, baptism Holy Spirit)

Baptism (Corporate) – The Greek word for baptize is baptizo (bap-tid'-zo), which means, "to make whelmed or fully wet." The root word for baptize is bapto, which means "to cover wholly with fluid." The corporate baptism is the submerging of those who are in corporate leadership within a local assembly. This baptism will bring the leadership into oneness and agreement of each other.

Baptism (Holy Spirit) – The baptism of the Holy Spirit is the full submerging into the Holy Spirit with evidence of speaking in tongues. The Believer is filled with the indwelling of the Holy Spirit. The believer just needs to receive the gift of the Holy Spirit by faith.

Baptism (Local Ministry) - The baptism of the Local Ministry is "the spiritual full immersion of the local corporate ministry into the Lord Jesus Christ." It is the baptism of our minds since they die only to be buried and then are resurrected into "one mind" which is the mind of Christ (Phil. 2:5). In the baptism of the local ministry, one's mentality must die in order that we may gain a corporate mentality of Christ. As we build God's physical house, our mentality must become corporate like His House. A local ministry cannot return to a mentality of separatism but must be changed into a corporate baptized mind of Christ. A baptized corporate mind will never return to the former things, for it is the former things that can kill a flow. The baptized local ministry must be smarter and use what is between their ears, which is the mind of Christ.

Barren – one who is unable to produce or yield a harvest. This speaks of someone who may be out of the perfect will of God.

Belial (spirit of) – The word Belial means "without profit, worthlessness, destruction or wickedness." The spirit of Belial is the spirit of wickedness, worthlessness and destruction, which seeks to operate in ministry. It is an anti-Excellence spirit that attempts to rule anywhere the order of the Lord is so that it can disrupt that order. The spirit of Belial will function amongst men and women in ministry who show no respect or regards to apostolic order within the priesthood.

Benjamin – the twelfth son of Jacob and father of the tribe of Benjamin. Next to Joseph, Benjamin was the favorite son. The name Benjamin means "son of my right hand." (Genesis 48:14). Next to Joseph, Benjamin was his favorite son of Jacob.

Beth- the second letter of the Hebrew alphabet, the word beth means "a house." The word beth alludes to a focal point of holiness, which is the house of God.

Birthright - special privileges and advantages belonging to the first-born son. In Jewish tradition the first born who had the birthright received a double portion of the father's goods. The Greek word for birthright is prototokia (pro-tot-ok'-ee-ah), which means "primogeniture." Primogeniture is "the state or fact of being the firstborn of children of the same parents. The believer today has a birthright and because of this standing also is to receive the double portion of the Fathers inheritance. (See double portion)

Bishoprick – The office of a bishop. Bishopric comes from the Greek word episcopos, which means "overseer or office." This word also means "to visit, inspect or to look over."

Bitter – a feeling of anger that is caused by a sharp piercing painful thought of a past issue that causes more distress by pondering on that particular thought. Bitter when displayed towards another individual will give the appearance of being vile and heartless.

Blood Covenant – The agreement between God and His people. The blood covenant goes as far back as Adam and the fall of man. The process of this type of covenant worked as follows, after the terms of the covenant were settled, an animal was divided in half through its median plane and laid out on the ground. Both parties would grasp hands, recite the terms and walk together between the pieces of the carcass. The blood covenant is the most serious and severe of all covenants. It signified that the party that broke the covenant would have the same thing done to them as to the animal. The blood covenant actually carried the death penalty. The terms of the blood covenant were permanent however the two parties could altar the covenant as long as both parties were alive, but once dead the terms of the blood covenant could not be changed. The blood according to Leviticus 17:11-12 atones for the human soul, it (the blood) communicates to God every thing there is to be known about the human being both physical and spiritual.

Brazen Altar - the altar of burnt offerings was also called the Brazen (Brass) Altar. The word altar comes from the Hebrew word mizbeach (miz-bay'-akh); its root word zabach (zaw-bakh') means, "to slaughter an animal (usually in sacrifice)." The Greek word for altar is thusiasterion (thoo-see-as-tay'-ree-on), which means "a place of sacrifice." The altar was an elevated place where the priest performed the sacrifice. The New Testament brazen altar is the cross.

Brazen Laver - a brass bowl that was to be filled with water. It was placed behind the altar but before the sanctuary (tent of meeting). The brazen laver was strictly for the priests to ceremoniously wash their hands and feet prior to entering the tabernacle. It is at the laver that one must understand the importance of the priest ministry within the local church. The brazen laver gives off a reflection of the Lord. As long as the preacher continues to be washed in the laver and look into the glass that holds the glory of the Lord, then he or she will continue to behold the glory of the Lord. Beholding the Lord means to really understand His will.

Burnt Offering - The burnt offering (Lev. 1:3) is called olah in the Hebrew, which means, "what goes up in smoke." The burnt offering was a sweet savour offering (Phil. 2:8). The burnt sacrifice was to be a male animal without blemish and served as a substitution for mans sins. The offerer placed his hand upon the animal to identify himself with the offering. This sacrifice denotes Jesus who voluntarily offered Himself without spot to God (Heb. 9:14). This offering represented the atonement for sin, enabling us who are not holy to approach a holy God.

Cain (spirit of) – Cain was the eldest son of Adam and Eve who followed the business of agriculture. The Lord rejected Cain's sacrifice but accepted his brother Abel's and because of this Cain slew his brother. In Genesis chapter four when the Lord approached Cain, he (Cain) responded, "Am I my brothers' keeper?" In the original it reads, "Am I the guard of my brother?" This is the position of the body of Christ; it is to guard one another. The spirit of Cain is the spirit of murder (character assassination) and also not guarding your brother leaving them exposed to the enemy. The spirit of Cain is brought on due to jealousy of another.

Candlestick – The candlestick (lampstand) stood in the inner sanctuary of the Tabernacle. It was of pure gold which and sat to the left of the table of incense and consisted of the base, shaft, and lamp. There were seven lamps (branches) to the one lampstand, three branches extended from one side of the center lamp and three from the other. The center lamp is Christ for He is seen in the midst of the seven candlesticks (Rev.1:13). The branches of the lamp projecting out of the lamp reveal ministries that must come out of or birthed through prayer out of the loins of Jesus (Acts 17:28; 1 Cor. 6:17). The candlestick represents the Light and the Truth and as the Light continuously burns it reveals continual Present Truth.

Carnal – fleshly or works of the flesh.

Carnality – works of the flesh attempting to operate in the Spirit

Cessationism – the teaching that denies the continuation of apostles after the death of the twelve (including Paul). The Cessationists argue that the gifts of the Spirit described in the New Testament ceased to exist when the apostles went off the scene.

Cessationists – one who holds to the teaching that apostles are no longer in existence today.

Charge – to transmit a message along from one to another. In 2 Timothy 6:13, Paul charged Timothy meaning he gave a transmitted a message from God to Timothy in regards to Timothy's call. A charge serves as apostolic instruction for kingdom work. It is instruction to the sons and daughters of kingdom.

Charity - love, affection or benevolence. This word in the Latin is caritas, which was used to translate the Greek word agape (ag-ah'-pay).

Chemosh – the god of the Moabites whom they worshiped as the war god. (Num. 21:29; Jer. 48:7, 13, 46). It is believed that Chemosh and Malik also known as Moloch is the same god. The bible reads in 1 Kings 11:7 that Solomon built a high place for Chemosh. (1 Kings 11:7). "For it came to pass, when Solomon was old, that his wives turned away his heart after other gods: and his heart was not perfect with the Lord his God, as was the heart of David his father." 1 Kings 11:4 This denotes a spirit which would causes someone seasoned to turn their heart away from God as Solomon did in his latter years. (See molechism).

Cheth - the eighth letter of the Hebrew alphabet, which means "a hedge." Jesus is our cheth or hedge. He is our protector.

Christology – the Greek word for Christ is Christos (khris-tos'), which means "anointed or anoint." This word is taken from the root word chrio, which means, "to smear or rub with oil." Christ is the anointed one; the word Christology is the study of Jesus Christ and His Anointing.

Church (The) - ekklesia (ek-klay-see'-ah) this word is made up of two words. The first is ek, which denotes origin (the point whence motion or action proceeds). The second word is kleo, which means to call. The word ekklesia means to call out or to call out from something where it originates. Where did it (the Church) originate? It originated in God so the Church is the called-out ones or the ones who were called out from God.

Coat (Broidered) - The broidered coat also known as a fringed tunic, was a basic garment over which the robe and ephod was worn by the priest. The word broidered is interpreted checkered; however, the root word means, "to interweave." This coat was a coat of many colors (Joseph's coat) that was woven together with various colors. This represents an anointing that enables the pastor to bring people together and work where there is unity amongst the brethren (Ps. 133:1). The broidered coat depicts an anointing of the spirit of unity that the pastor walks in and always administers.

Comforter - John 14:16 "And I will pray the Father, and he shall give you another Comforter, that he may abide with you for ever." The word comforter comes from the Greek word parakletos (par-ak'-lay-tos) which means an intercessor, advocate or consoler.

Commission – to give an authoritative order and charge that is to be done by the laying on of hands. Two things will transpire in commissioning; the first will be an impartation. Second there will be a releasing. The impartation is the kingdom authority that is released during the commissioning. The releasing is a releasing into kingdom work (1 Tim. 4:14). Such a commission can only be applied to those who are qualified and matured spiritually.

Common Hall - The Praetorium, the open courtyard or judgment hall (Matthew 27:26-27). This was Pilate's house and the camp headquarters of the Roman guard of the governor.

Communion – see the Lords table

Compassion – sympathy for the needs and problems of others

Confess – to fully agree in ones heart and speak out publicly that which is believed in the heart.

Confusion - one of the Hebrew words for confusion is hapher (khaw-fare'); which means "to be ashamed, disappointed or reproach". The Greek word is akatastasia (ak-at-as-tah-see'-ah), which means "instability, disorder, commotion, or tumult. Confusion is shame disappointment, reproach, disorder, commotion or tumult. In regards to ministry, confusion can lead to disorder however in regards to the enemy; confusion will bring disorder within the kingdom of darkness. The supernatural move of God creates confusion in the kingdom of darkness.

Convenience (spirit of) - The spirit of convenience is a spirit that does not call for sacrifice. It is anything that saves or simplifies work. It is a settling for what has been given or handed down by the enemy. It strives to keep individuals in their comfort zone never stepping out of the boat onto the water. It is the ease of doing that, which is likeable and doesn't require sacrifice.

Corinthian church - a church planted by Apostle Paul while on his second missionary journey to Corinth. He remained in Corinth a year and a half (Acts 18:11). This church was highly gifted however it needed much instruction on how to allow the gifts to operate in the church. The church at Corinth also battled with division, disorder, immorality, and false teaching concerning the resurrection (1 Cor. 15).

Courage - the attitude of facing and dealing with anything recognized as dangerous, difficult, or painful.

Covenant – a mutual understanding between two or more parties, each binding himself to fulfill specified obligations. The Old Testament word for covenant is beriyth (ber-eeth') which is primarily "a cutting", with reference to the custom of cutting or dividing animals in two and passing between the parts in ratifying a covenant.

Crucified – An execution in which a condemned person was affixed to a cross. In Galatians 2:20, Paul states he is crucified with Christ. The word crucified is the Greek word sustauroo (soos-tow-ro'-o). This word is a perfect tense verb, meaning it is an action that is completed in the past with ongoing results in the present. The crucifixion of Jesus took place in the past however the results of that crucifixion are ongoing even until this day.

Cupbearer – a person whose duty it was to serve the wine table of the king. This person held an important place of confidence with the king and was extremely trustworthy. Nehemiah was a cupbearer to Artaxerxes. Prophetically speaking, cupbearers are worship leaders within the kingdom whose job it is to prepare and taste of the worship prior to it being offered up to the Lord.

Curse – to speak of doom over someone or something.

Daleth - the fourth letter of the Hebrew alphabet, which means "a door or a gate." Prophetically, the daleth speaks of Jesus being our open door or entranceway to the Father.

Dan - Son of Jacob and Bilhah (Rachel's maidservant) and father of the tribe of Dan and one of the twelve tribes of Israel. Dan was one of the brothers involved in the plot to sell Joseph into slavery.

Deborah – prophetess and judge of Israel also known as the Mother of Israel. Deborah had many accomplishments and among them she led the armies of Israel in battle. Her prophetic songs serve as a means of encouragement to many.

Demon - The Greek word for demon is daimon and daimonion. It is derived from the word daio, which means, "to divide" or "apportion." Demons are an evil spirit better known as familiar spirits that are sent by the enemy to bring division, inflict suffering and pain on powerless people or people who fail to understand the authority that they have over demonic forces. Demons are unclean spirits able to influence.

Demotion –the act of self-placement placing oneself lower than what God has called an individual into. This type of believer is one who lacks confidence and faith in who God has made them to be. (See Promotion)

Devils – spiritual authorities, territorial princes over various regions throughout the earth.

Devil (the) – Satan, the prince and the power of the air, the god of this word. He was Lucifer son of the morning, an anointed cherub (Isaiah 14:12, Ezek. 28:14)

Diadem – a piece of cloth, which at times was studded with gems worn as a head-dress for a king or queen. It was also known as the mitre, which was the headdress of the high Priest. Jesus is our high priest crowned with the diadem of glory and honor (Psalm 8:5).

Diana (the goddess) - One of the Seven Wonders of the World was considered to be in Ephesus. It was the temple Artemis, better known as the temple of the goddess Diana. Artemis was her Greek name while Diana was her Roman name. Silversmiths had a prosperous business selling silver shrines and images of Diana (Acts 19:24-35). This image was to the Romans one of the most sacred images in the ancient world. It was not a beautiful image; it depicted Diana as a lewd goddess having four rows of breasts. This goddess denotes a spirit of prostitution. According to Acts 19:24-35, the city encouraged much trade, because of the legalized prostitution.

Dinahism - Dinah was the daughter of Jacob and Leah; she was the 7th child and only daughter of Leah. Dinah wondered away from her father Jacobs's house to attend an ungodly Canaanite Festival, which celebrated the god of nature. When she wondered away from her father's house she was raped. Dinahism denotes the spirit of wonder or wondering away from the Lord. It is an unsettled spirit desiring to taste a part of the world. Curiosity is seen in the spirit of Dinahism because it causes one to become curious concerning the things of the world, the end thereof is a trap by the enemy. (See Schechem the spirit)

Divination (spirit of) - the word divination is the Greek word Puthon (poo'-thone) and is derived from the word Putho. Putho was the name of the region where Delphi the seat of a famous oracle (a person through whom spirits are to believed speaks through) was located. In Acts 16:16 where it reads "a certain damsel possessed with a spirit of divination" should read a certain damsel possessed with the spirit of python. The word divination actually means python. The spirit of python (divination) denotes one who operates demonically being utilized by demonic forces in order to give information. This type spirit is found in areas of those seeking horoscopes, tarot card, and astrologers. This spirit is released into individuals who seek for answers other than finding them in the Word of God. (see witchcraft, sorcery)

Divine Impartation – a transmittal of anointed ability that enables the believer to manifest kingdom results. (See impartation)

Divine Order – Gods divine accurate unchangeable arrangement in regards to His purpose that cannot be altered.

Double Portion - the double portion is a double portion of goods the first-born is to receive from his father.

Double Portion Anointing – the double portion anointing operates on sons and daughters of spiritual fathers and mothers. When a son or a daughter takes over or continues a vision they receive the double portion anointing. The double portion anointing is the anointing of the spiritual father or mother in order to continue the work, and they receive the portion of anointing from the Father who anoints them to take the vision to another dimension thereby receive two or a double portion of anointing.

Eagle – the eagle throughout scripture denotes the symbol of the prophet. The Latin term for the name Aquila mentioned in Acts 18:2 means eagle.

Edenic Covenant – the covenant God made with Adam and Eve in the Garden of Eden before the fall and entrance into sin.

Edifying – this word means architecture, which denotes designing and structure. Edifying speaks of designing and structuring or building up.

Eight – the number eight denotes new beginnings and dedication. The 8th chapter of Genesis reads that after the flood Noah began civilization all over again. Leviticus 9:1 opens with "the eighth day." Holy Convocation was to begin on the eighth day. In Scripture an eight-day period was always the pattern of dedication. The Feast of Tabernacles is a feast day, which speaks of the eighth day. When Ahaz's son King Hezekiah came to the throne he cleansed the Temple and rededicated it to the Lord after eight days (2 Chron. 29:16-17). The Feast of Passover was an eight-day celebration that revealed a new season.

Ek-klessia – (See Church The)

Elders – represent the government of the local church. Elders operate under the umbrella of which and who ordained them. If an apostle ordains then they (elders) operate under an apostolic anointing. The umbrella and anointing in which elders operate under is important because it is those elders who will assist in the direction of the local church. Both ears and hearts of the elder must be circumcised and as the apostles lay hands upon them and give them to the Lord, circumcision takes place.

Elijah - a prophet who stood before King Ahab and prophesied that there would be no rain for three years. He is considered one of the greatest prophets that walked the face of this earth.

Elisha – spiritual son of Elijah and also the successor of Elijah who received the mantle of Elijah. Elisha is the only prophet where the bible specifically documents that he died from a terminal illness. Prior to his death king Joash mourned over Elisha while weeping "My father, my father the chariot of Israel and horsemen thereof." Those were the same words Elisha mourned when his spiritual father Elijah was taken up in a whirlwind.

Emulation (spirit of) – the spirit of jealousy

Enmity – hostility or hatred.

Ephesus (the church) - The name Ephesus means, "To let go, to relax." The city of Ephesus was the capitol of heathen idolatry and it was from Ephesus that idolatry would spread all over the world. The apostle Paul spent over 2 years in Ephesus and while there was used by the Holy Spirit to break the power of darkness and lead souls to Christ, causing many to leave the idolatrous worship and superstitions of Ephesus. After Paul, came John who lived in Ephesus for about 30 years, and made this city the headquarters for his work of the Lord Jesus Christ. The Church at Ephesus had good works and was a working church. In Revelation chapter two, the Lord spoke of the Ephesus church, He knew of their labors. They were patient and showed their patience towards the weaker Christians. They had "tried" those that said they were apostles and but found them to be liars. Ephesus looked upon the name of Jesus as the name above every name. They walked in love and developed the fruit of the Spirit. It began as a charismatic church but Jesus was looking at them some forty years later. It was a second and third generation church and He saw their labor, faithfulness and discipline. They hated the things that Jesus hated but they lost their first love, they had fallen. The Church at Ephesus was admonished to repent and do their first work over. The reward for their obedience was that they would eat of the tree of life. (See Smyrna, Laodicea, Philadelphia, Sardis, Thyatira, Pergamos)

Ephod - a two-piece, sleeveless apron worn by the priest. This apron depicts one as being a servant and it represents the spirit and anointing of servanthood.

Ephraim (son of Joseph) - Ephraim was the brother of Manasseh, and the son of Joseph. Jacob adopted Ephraim and Manasseh as part of the tribe of Simeon and Reuben. Ephraim received the blessing of the firstborn, although Manasseh was the eldest, because Jacob foresaw that Ephraim's ancestors would be greater than his brother's (Genesis 48:13-20).

Eschewed evil – departs from or avoids evil?

Evangelist - Messenger of good tidings; a preacher of the Gospel. An evangelist is one of the five-fold ministry gifts. The Evangelist ministry operates in the power gifts, which are gift of faith, working of miracles and gifts of healings. These gifts are supernaturally activated by the Spirit of God to function upon the Evangelist.

Evil – that which is dysfunctional and wicked.

Exator Mortis - When Jesus was taken to be beaten there were four Roman Soldiers lead by a fifth Roman Soldier. The fifth soldier was known as an Exator Mortis. The Exator Mortis was the one who did the whipping. The five men were specially trained in crucifixion procedures and techniques. The Exator Mortis' job was to weaken the victim and to break his will but not under any circumstances to kill him. If the Exator Mortis killed the victim the he was made to be a substitute for the victim therefore the Exator Mortis became experts at keeping their victims alive.

Excellence - From the word excellence comes the word excel which means "to be better or greater or superior to another or others." It implies superiority in some quality, skill, or achievement. To excel means to surpass, and it implies surpassing or going beyond the norm in quality: Excellence is the mindset and means of functioning in both the believer and the local church. It means that you give it your best and because of excellence your best goes beyond the norm in quality.

Exhorter – one who encourages the people of God.

Eyesalve – medicine for the eyes. Prophetically speaking it speaks of spiritual medicine that removes the scales from ones eyes. It causes the believer to walk in the spirit of revelation. Eyesalve denotes moving into a higher realm seeing God fully in a greater and deeper way.

Ezra - Ezra was a scribe and priest who lived during the time of Artaxerxes. He was a ready scribe in the Law of Moses. What is a ready scribe? It is one who is skillful in writing, communicating the history and Word of the Lord. Ezra was responsible for leading many of the Israelites from Babylon to Jerusalem. (See Scribe)

Faith –The Old Testament word for faith or faithful means to stand firm, to trust, to be certain, to believe in. Another word for faith is trust which means 'to run to the shelter of a rock or a mother bird's wings for shelter.' If one trusts something they can run to it. The New Testament word for faith is pisteo which means an action based upon a belief. Faith is running to that which you believe. (See trust)

Farthing - A small coin nearly equal to a half-penny of our money.

Fast - means to cover over the mouth. Psalms 35:13 reads "I humbled my soul with fasting." A fast is necessary for the operation of apostolic ministry for in Acts 13:1-4, the apostles received instruction for ordination through fasting.

Father (Spiritual) – The word father literally means "one who gives strength to the family." A spiritual father is one who is able to give strength (insight) to a spiritual son or daughter.

Fear of the Lord – the reverence and respect towards God by the believer.

Feast Days - The Feasts constitute a type of pattern for the church. In order to understand this pattern, it will require a consecrated walk in the Holy Spirit that He might release into you the revelation of the pattern. The Feasts typify the church age and unveils God's will for the church. There were three Feasts: the Feasts of Passover, the Feast of Pentecost, and the Feast of Tabernacles. These Feasts consisted of seven major events, three that comprised the feast of the Passover. One Feast which stood alone (the Feast of Pentecost), and then the remaining three events comprised the Feast of Tabernacles. (see passover, unleavened bread, firstfruits, Pentecost, day of the trumpet, day of atonement, feast of Tabernacles)

Feast of Tabernacles – the feast of tabernacles is called Sukkot in the Hebrew and is sometimes referred to as the Feast. This feast began on the 15th day of the month of Tishri (September-October) which was five days after the Day of Atonement and lasted for seven days. The Feast of Tabernacles consisted of the Israelites dwelling in the sukkah (singular for booths) or tents and celebrating God's provision.   Prophetically, the Feast of Tabernacle is a time of restoration and reaping a harvest of all that had been planted; a harvest of blessing, prayers, and, most importantly, a harvest of souls. (See Passover, unleavened bread, firstfruits, Pentecost, day of the trumpet, Day of Atonement, feast of Tabernacles)

Firmament - The Hebrew word for firmament is raqiya` (raw-kee'-ah) which comes from the root word raqa` which means to hammer out. The word firmament denotes something that was flat; it denotes space, atmosphere, expanse or an opening.

First - taken from the Greek word proton, which means being first in time, place, order, or importance as a matter of relevance. The apostle is mentioned as the first gift in 1 Cor. 12: 28.

Firstfruits (The Sheaf - Feast of) - the celebration involved taking one sheaf (10%) of the harvest crop and waving it before the Lord. This festival took place on the 16th day of the first month. The number 16 is the number for resurrection. Keep in mind: the Passover took place on the 14th night (the day of preparation, Luke 23:53-54). The festival of Unleavened Bread was celebrated on the 15th day while the Sheaf of Firstfruits was celebrated on the 16th day. There are to be noticed three days: the 14th, 15th and 16th. These three days represent the resurrection of Christ. (See Passover, unleavened bread)

Five Fold Ministry (The Hand of the Lord) - The hand of the Lord represents the five-fold ministry, which is the extended right hand of the Lord. Each finger on the hand denotes one gift of the five-fold ministry. The Lord's thumb represents the gift of apostleship. The second finger represents the prophet; the third finger represents the evangelist; the fourth finger represents the pastor and the smallest and last finger represents the gift of teacher. The five-fold ministry is the element God uses on earth to build up and direct the body of Christ as a whole.

Flagrum (or Plumbatae in the Latin) - The Roman whip used to beat Jesus. This whip was Roman whip that consisted of 3 leather thongs attached to a wooden handle. Each leather thong had at least a single dumbbell shaped piece of bone or lead attached to the end of it. (See Exator Mortis, whipping post)

Fool – From the Hebrew word nabal (naw-bawl'), which means "stupid or wicked"

Foot washing - At the Last Supper, Jesus washed the disciples' feet. Feet washing denote the symbol of servanthood and humility.

Forbearance – Patience, slow anger and self-restraint. Forbearance speaks of ones attitude towards others who have not matured.

Former Rain - a season of rain that prepares the ground. The former rain is also called an early or seed rain. This is a rain for preparation. The former rain also denotes a former rain word that is a word of preparation for what God is getting ready to release. (See latter rain)

Fret (not) – The word fret is the Hebrew word charah (khaw-raw') which means "to become warm, blaze up of anger, zeal, jealousy to be angry." The bible reads in Psalm 37:8, "Cease from anger, and forsake wrath: fret not thyself in any wise to do evil." Fret not meaning don't become warm or blazed up with anger, zeal or jealousy. Don't allow yourself to be placed in a position that will cause you to fret and in turn cause you to seek to do evil.

Fruit of the Spirit – The Nine fruit of the Spirit are found in Galatians 5:22-23, they denote the Character of God. The nine fruit of the Spirit are love, joy, peace, longsuffering, gentleness, goodness, faith, meekness and temperance.

Frustrate - frustrate is the Hebrew word 'aphec (aw-face') which means, "to cause to disappear, cease, be gone (at an end brought to naught), fail." This is the trick and trap of the enemy which means to frustrate the believers vision, to cause it to disappear, cease, be gone, come to naught and fail however the Life of God will give you power to overcome.

Furlong – denotes measurement of approximately 660 feet.

Gad - the seventh son of Jacob and father of the tribe of Gad. Gad was one of the twelve tribes of Israel. His mother was Zilpah, Jacob's concubine and Leah's slave. Gad's name comes from the Hebrew word troop. He was part of the plot to sell Joseph to Egypt and later sent to Egypt to buy corn during the famine in Canaan.

Gainsaying – the act of answering negatively, to speak against. Gainsaying also denotes disobedience.

Gamaliel (Gamliel) – In Acts 22:3 Paul states that he was a Jew born in Tarsus at the feet of Gamaliel. Gamaliel was also known as Gamaliel Ha-Zaken (the Elder). He was a Pharisee and member of the Sanhedrin. His learning was so eminent, and his character so revered, that he is one of the seven who alone among Jewish doctors have been honored with the title of "Rabban (master-teacher). Gamaliel was the person who wisely pleaded the cause of Peter and the other apostles in Acts 5:34-40, It is believed that Gamaliel was one for reform especially for regulations designed to protect the rights of women and sought for regulations to improve society. Scholars believe that Gamaliel died embracing the Christian faith and prior to his death remained a member of the Sanhedrin for the purpose of secretly helping his fellow-Christians. Gamaliel died around the time that James the Just was martyred

Genesis - received its English name from the Greek translation of the Hebrew word toledot, which is used thirteen times in Genesis and is translated as "story" (Gen. 2:4), record (5:1), or "line" (10:1). In Hebrew the name of this book is called bereishit, which means "In the beginning."

Gentiles – a nation of people other than Israel.

Gershonites – an order of the priesthood who were in charge of the fabrics of the tabernacle when it was moved from place to place, the curtains, veils, and tent-hangings. (See Merarites, Levites, Gershonites, Kohathites)

Gifts of the Spirit – The nine gifts of the spirit denoted the ministry of God. Those gifts are: word of wisdom, word of knowledge, faith, gifts of healing, working of miracles, prophecy, discerning of spirits, divers kinds of tongues and the interpretation of tongues (1 Cor. 12:8-10). The nine gifts of the spirit are divided into three divisions: the revelational gifts, power gifts, and oral gifts. (See revelational, power and oral gifts)

Gimel – the third letter of the Hebrew alphabet which means "to nourish until completely ripe." Prophetically gimel speaks of maturity.

Gird – to prepare, equip or secure. Prophetically gird means to prepare oneself in the spirit.

Girdle - The girdle was an ornamental belt that kept every article of the garments in place. Revelation 1:13 reads: "And in the midst of the seven candlesticks one like unto the Son of man, clothed with a garment down to the foot, and girt about the paps with a golden girdle." During those days, men who wore girdles around the paps or chest area were recognized as judges and lawyers. The type of girdle is what displays the type of office. The girdle went around the waste of the priest and was responsible for keeping all other articles of clothing in place. The girdle prophetically denotes the spirit of order and character.

Glory – the Old Testament word for glory is kabowd (kaw-bode'), which means weight or weighty, splendor or honor. The New Testament word for glory is doxa, which speaks of splendor or brightness. Glory speaks of the weighty splendor and brightness of the Lord that appears as a result of praise and worship.

Goats Hair – the second type of covering mentioned in the tabernacle of Moses. Goat's hair was woven into the linen fabric and served as a covering for the inner court. Eleven curtains forty-five feet long by six feet wide were sewn together in two sets. One set consisted of 5 curtains while the other consisted of six. The set of six covered the top and sides of the Holy Place, with the sixth curtain visible to all and doubled in the front of the building (East Side). The set of the Five covered the sides of the Holy of Holies as well as the rear wall of the tabernacle. Both sets were joined together by one hundred blue loops and fifty brass clasps, and this connection was directly over the veil that separated the Holy Place and the Holy of Holies. The goat's hair being interwoven with the linen denotes a type of prevailing prayer, which is warfare prayer. This prayer must continually be mentioned within the sanctuary. (See Rams skins, Badgers skins)

Godly Covenant Principle – The Godly covenant principle is God's covenant to His people. It reveals how God obligated Himself and sealed it by making an oath. It is a major vehicle in which God expresses His love for His people and in turn gives the believers a desire of obligation towards God. (See covenant)

Gospel – The Greek word euaggelion (yoo-ang-ghel'-ee-on) that means "good message" or "good news." Paul in Romans 1:16 reads "For I am not ashamed of the gospel of Christ: for it is the power of God unto salvation to every one that believeth; to the Jew first, and also to the Greek." The Gospel is the good news of God displayed in the full power and demonstration of God to all who believe.

Grace – the unearned favor of the Lord extended towards His people.

Grave clothes – Primary burial clothing used to bury biblical individuals. The clothing consisted of three articles

- Sindon - which is a large linen sheet, which the body was laid in.
- Othonia - The Linen cloth or burial strips, which were used to bind the hands and feet.
- Sudarion – a face cloth to cover the face or the mouth.

Prophetically speaking, grave clothes denotes the clothing the enemy attempts to place on the believer. The Sindon serves as the enemy's attempt to bind an individual. The Othonia denotes the enemy's attempt to bind your hand so that you cannot work in the kingdom and to bind your feet so that you cannot walk in the things of God. The enemy attempts to cover you with the Sudarion so that you cannot speak of the things of God. However Jesus went to the grave of Lazarus and after Jesus called Lazarus forth, Jesus stated, "Lose him and let him go." What the enemy attempts to bind the believer with, Jesus is saying Loose you and let you go.

Guile (spirit of) – the spirit of guile is the spirit of deceit and craftiness. It speaks of one devising a plan in order to deceive an individual.

Hananiah (spirit of) – The spirit of Hananiah is the spirit of a false prophet who causes God's people to believe in false hope. In Jeremiah 28, Hananiah prophesied that the captivity would be over within two years which was not so, and he caused the people to believe, he gave them a false hope. The false prophecy resulted in Hananiah dying in that same year in the seventh month.

Hand Covenant - Much like the handshake of today, two parties would shake hands or strike the palms of their hands together. (Ezra 10:19; Ezek. 17:18)

He - the fifth letter of the Hebrew alphabet which denotes an opening meaning a window. He is the window of heaven used by the Father to pour out blessings upon His people.

Hebrew - `Ibriy (ib-ree'). The word eber comes from the root word `eber (ay'-ber) which means, "to cross over." The word Hebrew refers to one who has crossed over into covenant. The believer today is also one who has "crossed over" into covenant.

Hebrew Praise Words

- **Barak**- in 2 Chron. 6:13, Solomon made the brazen scaffold, stood upon it then kneeled down. The Hebrew word kneeled is *barak* (baw-rak') which means "to bend the knee in homage or to drink water. It also denotes the idea of presenting a gift or giving honor to another. Barak also has a two-fold meaning which means to bless and to curse. When one baraks they bless God and at the same time curse the enemy. Everyone baraks to something, either your blessing God or your blessing the enemy. All of the Hebrew praise words culminate in the Hebrew praise word barak for it is the ultimate place where both praise and worship leads us. Barak is a position that cannot be compromised; it is a position of brokenness, faithfulness, confidence, honor, glory, adoration, humility and worship. Barak denotes a position where you bless God for all that He was, is, and forever shall be. Barak is third dimensional worship, in other words, it's a realm whereas no one or nothing matters but God. The Body of Christ as a whole must come to this posture of ba-rak. Barak does not call for a vocal praise but does call for a bowing in His presence and keeping silent so that the Father may speak to one's heart. To barak Him means to bow the knee however the heart must bow as well and when one does not they mark God. 2 Chr. 6:13

Halal - to raise your hands as a sign of surrender looking to be lead out. This word in its original concrete meaning is a bright light that guides the journey and we "halal" Yah by looking at Him to guide us on our journey through life.

Hilluwl – This word means "To be merry" and it denotes a time of celebration of a harvest. Prophetically *hilluwl* means "to become the praise of the Lord and in that praise Him for breakthrough and harvest."

Mahalal - To praise or to boast or shine before the Lord through one's praise. "As the fining pot for silver and the furnace for gold; so is a man to his praise [*mahalal*]." (Prov. 27:21)

Mechowlah – this word denotes a company of dancers whereas many dancing appear as one. *Mechowlah* is a corpo-rate dance in the spirit realm revealing a corporate adoration for what the Lord has done.

Nagad - to declare or stand boldly in His presence with your arms uplifted in order to testify or declare the wonder-ful works of God.

`Oz – an action of praise which will produce physical might or strength. (Psalms 29:11)

Pacach – this word means "to literally skip or to hop over." This is a dance of deliverance where the people of God do not allow the enemy to hold them down with troubles but to *pacach* or skip over what the enemy attempts to present to God's people.

Raqad- To properly stamp or to spring about wildly for joy, to trample the ground with one's feet. *Raqad* denotes a dance of victory. The bible reads that the enemy is under your feet and through one's victory dance as my feet trample the ground they are actually trampling the enemy's head.

Ron – To rejoice, a shout of joy, a shout of deliverance.

32

- **Ruwa`**- To shout with a sound that splits the ears. In Joshua 6:20, when the people heard the sound of the trumpet they *ruwa'* or shouted so loud that it split the ears of the enemy.

Dan. 2:23
- **Shabach**- To get a full understanding of the word *shabach* one must look at its action. The action of this word denotes movement with the arm. It is a stroking movement in order to soothe. The soothing denotes peace. The word *shabach* means to praise the Lord in order to bring peace or a soothing. The believer in there praise has the ability to praise God until the peace of God is released into a situation. The Father calms and soothes us through glorifying Him. The shabach of the individual is able to bring a soothing and a glorifying of Him and the situation. *Shabach* means to praise Him in order to bring peace, soothing and calmness to your situation.

- **Shevach** - to honor and adore. The driving force of one's praise is their *shevach* which speaks of one honoring and adoring Him.

1 Chr. 6:32
13:8 →
Blow the trumpet →
Ps. 47:1 →
81:3
- **Shiyr** - to sing and walk and move minstrelsy.
- **Taga'** – To clap by means of slapping or bringing hands together. Taga' is the clapping or the slapping together of the hands denoting an in outward expression of joy because of indwelling of the praise in the heart of the believer.

- **Tanah** – the root of this word means "that which is brought to a harlot. The idea means to give or attribute honor. The word *tanah* denotes something of value that is brought to someone as a gift as a means of praise in order to honor. In Judges 5:11, they rehearsed or expressed their honor of the righteous acts of the Lord.

Ps. 22:3
Ps. 34:1
- **Tehillah** - a hymn of praise, a song of the Lord, a song from the Lord. Prophetically speaking, the word *tehillah* is a clear, crisp, sharp song, coming from you unto the Lord. It is the sound unto the Lord that is released from you unto Him. It is the clear crisp, sharp song that God has given you.

Ps. 22:7
Ps. 50:14,23
- **Towdah** – the extending of the hand in order to confess. The praise of confession or *towdah* also speaks of the sacrifice of praise. The Father has made us His confession. We confess our sin, then we become His confession in worship

Thanksgiving

33

and speak or towdah his marvelous works. This praise is both seen and heard by the hands being extended or lifted.

- **Yadah** – this word means, "To give thanks." The root of this word is *yad*, which denotes the hand. *Yad* also involves the moving and extending of the hand. The movement of the hand is depicted with its action of the hand. It involves making a motion as to throw a stone or an arrow. The word *yadah* speaks of the throwing forth of the hand by motioning to throw a stone or an arrow. *Halel* shows us the direction, which the service is to go. After the Lord reveals the direction of the service then it is time to *yadah* the Lord, to make an action of throwing forth the hands as to throw something i.e. an arrow or stone. In the Spirit realm, the *yadah* releases spiritual arrows into the atmosphere in order to break up any type of hindrances or clouds from the enemy. The praise must be thrown into the atmosphere at the enemy however, at the same time we are telling God thanks. The word *yadah* also means to yield to one's authority.

- **Yacaph** –Psalm 71:14 "But I will hope continually, and will yet praise thee more and more." The words more and more are one word in the Hebrew, which is *yacaph*. *Yacaph* means, "To add to your praise" and "to give a fresh praise continually."

- **Zamar** – The root word of *zamar* means "to pluck." The word describes the action of striking or plucking an instrument by using the fingers like striking a guitar. In Matthew 12:1 Jesus plucked the ears of the corn to get something to eat. David in the book of 2 Sam. 23 wanted something to drink. David denotes the Father desiring water, which means worship. In Matthew Jesus plucked the ears of the corn. The instrument is that which is plucked, strung or pulled on. You the believer are the instrument or the *zamar* of the Lord. By him plucking or pulling on you means that He calls upon the believer to play Him a melody. We are His *Zamar* and are fine tuned by the Father.

- **Zimrah** - a musical piece or song to be accompanied by an instrument. Not only has the Father made us His instrument but has also given us a song to go along with that instrument.

Handwritten margin notes:
1 Chr. 23:30
29:13
* 2 Chr. 5:13ff
Ps. 30:12

34

Heil (the spirit of) – Heil was the Bethelite who laid the foundation for the rebuilding of Jericho. Approximately 500 years previously, Joshua had decreed that any person who attempts to rebuild Jericho would be cursed. The spirit of Heil denotes a spirit that attempts to pull up, rebuild or reestablish something that God had already dealt with and destroyed. This spirit attempts to revert to the past life of a believer and attempts to resurrect that past life.

High Priest – The Old Testament High priest order began with Aaron. The high priest's main duties, in addition to the duties of a regular priest, were to perform the service of the Day of Atonement; to inquire God's will by the Urim and Thummim in the breastplate of his office, and to offer the sacrifices on Sabbaths, new moons, and yearly festivals. The position of the high priest was hereditary and also a lifetime calling and when rightly appointed was by divine influence of God. Today, Jesus Christ is our Great High Priest. All other high priest prior to Jesus simply served as pre-figures. In scripture our High priest is noted as a merciful and faithful High priest (Heb. 2:17), the high priest of our confession (Heb. 3:1), the great high priest who has passed through the heavens (Heb. 4:14), our high priest who can sympathize with our weaknesses (Heb. 4:15).

Holy – to be cut out and separated from someone to someone.

Holy of Holies - The Holy of Holies also known as The Most Holy Place was the third room of the tabernacle of Moses located behind the Sanctuary. In order to get to the third room one had to pass through the veil. All three rooms had entrances. The Outer Court had a gate, the Inner Court had a curtain (door), and the Holy of Holies had a veil. The Holy of Holies was the third room that represented the third level or the third dimension. It was in this room in which the glory of God appeared. Since this room housed the glory, it was important that the priest be covered in the blood and stood before the incense. The third room denotes a third level of praise, which is worship; it speaks of a level of perfection and maturity.

Hope - To hope means to know or have confidence in. (See faith, trust)

Ichabod – Name meaning no glory, the glory of the Lord has departed.

Idol – image worshipped in the place of God

Idolatry – the practice of idol worship

Immutability – the unchangeableness of God. Immutability speaks of one who is not a turncoat, or one who absolutely does not change. His word is unchanging, and His position as to His promise does not change. Immutability refers to the Father who has made a promise and will stand by that promise. (See oath)

Impartation – a transmittal of ability (see divine impartation)

Incarnate – the Latin word for incarnate means enfleshment. When incarnate is mentioned it speaks of Christ putting on human flesh with His divine person and becoming man; a Divine Person united to a human nature.

Incense –the incense was a mixture of gums or spices and the like, used for the purpose of producing a perfume when burned. It was used during the Old Testament sacrifices and offerings. The incense fumigated the sanctuary and by doing so would over ride the odor of the dead sacrifices. Its ingredients were distinct and needed to be searched for because they were not common. Those ingredients for the incense were stacte, onycha, galbanum and frankincense. Stacte was a gum of a storax tree found in the Middle East (it speaks of rescue, salvation, and deliverance). Onycha was oil that came from a shellfish (this speaks of total death) which was found on the shores of the Red Sea and the Indian Ocean. It is said to increase the fragrance of other perfumes and to be the base of perfumes made in the East Indies. Galbanum is the juice of a shrub that grew in Arabia, Persia, India and Africa. The shrub was to be broken in order to get the juice (this speaks of a vessel becoming broken). Frankincense is the most important of aromic gems and is regarded by itself as a precious perfume or a volatile oil. Frankincense was what caused the smoke to turn white (this speaks of holiness). Salt was also added to the incense, and it represents incorruption. The incense is made up of four ingredients, which describes the life and testimony of a believer; being found (salvation), total death (complete submission), brokeness (true worship), and holiness (character of God). The believer receives salvation and then goes through the process of complete submission (this is total death to the flesh). As the Galbanum was to be broken in order to get the juice out of it, so must the believer become broken in order that God might get all of the glory out of ones life. The fourth ingredient represents holiness, which is the character of God that becomes the character of the believer (1 Peter 1:16). The priest went into the Holy of Holies with incense. He would put the incense in the censer (a bowl) that was full of hot coals using his right hand (the hand of authority). The incense going on the hot coals would cause a cloud to appear. The cloud of the incense served as a type of screen between the Shekinah Glory of God and the priest who was offering up the incense. Had the priest encountered the glory without the incense, he would have died. The coals that ignited the incense came from the brazen altar of sacrifice in the outer court because the fire that is upon the brazen altar ignited everything in the tabernacle. The believers with testimonies become the incense of God. The hot coals represent the life of prayer. Prayer (coals) with incense (testimony) produces a smoke (praise). Once the believer operates in this realm of praise, God releases glory. Incense is the praise that comes up out of the believer. The incense that God called for is the praise that burns upon the altar.

Inner Court - The second room of the tabernacle of Moses was also referred to as the Inner Court or Sanctuary. The items in this room consisted of a candlestick, á table of Shewbread, and a table of incense. Daily, the priest entered the sanctuary and their jobs were to offer incense at the time of morning and evening prayer, renew the lights on the golden lampstand; and, on the Sabbath, the priests were to remove the old Shewbread and replace it with new Shewbread on the table. All priests who offered up offerings within the tabernacle practiced this constant duty and their practices became their way of living. Prophetically speaking the Inner Court denotes the second dimension or second level of maturity and in that dimension the believer begins to understand their purpose and prepare for it. It is at this point in the life and walk of the believer that Christ begins to reveal to leadership the mysteries of His will (Eph.1: 9). The second room is not just a room but denotes a higher level of functioning, a higher level of attitude, a higher level of dedication and commitment, and, most importantly, a time of preparation to get ready to become the completed person whom God has ordained.

Inspiration - This word is from the Greek word theopneustos (theh-op'-nyoo-stos) which is made up of two words Theos which means God and pneo which means breathed. The word inspiration means God breathed or divinely breathed.

Integrity – Integrity is "the quality or state of being complete, unbroken, and whole." It is an adherence to moral and ethical principles; soundness of moral character; honesty. Integrity is noted at times of suffering great adversity and is displayed in those who function in apostolic anointing and kingdom work. Integrity distinguishes between true and false men and women of God.

Iraq – is identified in the Bible as Babylon, Land of Shinar, and Mesopotamia.

Isaac – the son of Abraham through Sarai who was the son of the promise. (Gen. 22:1-14). Isaac denotes the Church.

Isaiah – One of the greatest Old Testament prophets to ever prophesy. The Hebrew name means "Salvation of Jehovah." He prophesied concerning Judah and Jerusalem in the days of Uzziah, Jotham, Ahaz and Hezekiah, kings of Judah. He was the first major prophet responsible for leaving behind prophetic writings. He was called the Messianic prophet because of him foreseeing and foretelling of Christ's coming. The book of Isaiah contains sixty-six chapters, which are the same amount of books in the KJV Bible. Isaiah was married and had two sons. Tradition states that at around the age of 90, King Manasseh had Isaiah executed by having him placed in the trunk of a tree and having him sawn asunder.

Ishmael – the son of Abraham through Hagar. Ishmael was the son of the flesh and not of the promise. Prophetically Ishmael denotes operating in the flesh in order to produce the desire of the flesh, it is a man-made attempt to bring forth the promises of God.

Israel – the biblical patriarch Jacob whose name was changed to Israel after he wrestled with the angel. The name Israel means "he will rule as God." Jacob blessed his twelve sons and prophesied to them concerning their destinies. The descendants of Jacob are called Israelites or in the Hebrew Bene Israel meaning "Children of Israel." (See Jacob)

Issachar – One of the twelve sons of Jacob and the fifth son of Leah. The name Issachar means, "he will bring a reward" which was due to the fact that Leah feeling that God had rewarded her with her son Issachar. In the last words of Jacob to his sons he speaks of Issachar as being a strong ass couching down between two burdens (Gen. 49:14). This denotes Issachar's great strength and ability to carry burdens. It also speaks of Issachar's desire to couch down or delight in the restfulness of a rural life.

Ithamar – the youngest son of Aaron who was to oversee the Gershonites and the Merarites priests who had the responsibility of transporting the tabernacle. Eli the High Priest came through the family of Ithamar.

Jabez – Not much is known of Jabez. He was a descendant of Judah (1Chr. 4:9-10) and he wrote a prayer that consisted of four requests that God granted.

Jabez (the prayer) - one verse prayer, with four requests, granted by God.

Jacob – The third of the biblical patriarchs and the son of Isaac and Rebekah. The name Jacob means heel catcher or a supplanter. He was a trickster as he tricked his twin brother Esau into giving up his birthright and afterward, acquired the blessing. Jacob married Leah and Rachel On his deathbed Jacob prophesied to his twelve sons and in that prophecy he was able to describe the characters of each son both positive and negatively. (See Israel)

Jahaziel - The son of Zechariah who was also a prophet. He prophesied to Jehoshaphat and the Children of Israel in 2 Chronicles 20:15 "for the battle is not yours, but God's."

Jannes and Jambres (spirit of) – two people who opposed Moses. The spirit of Jannes and Jambres is the spirit of opposition against apostolic anointing. It also denotes the spirit of defiance and disobedience that will eventually lead to the spirit of witchcraft.

Jaziz - A Hagarite who was over the flocks of King David. This name denotes the spirit of stewardship. In stewardship an individual is given something to take care of or tend to. In regards to leadership pastors are God's Jaziz whereas the flock of God is entrusted to them.

Jehu (spirit of) – Jehu was a prophet of God who pronounced judgment upon the king of Israel Baasha. The spirit of Jehu is the spirit of boldness of a prophet who is obedient to the Father and will say whatever the Father speaks. (See Baasha)

Jephthah – one of the Judges of Israel who was first considered an outcast by his half brothers. Jephthah left and went to a place called Tob where he became the head of a band of mercenaries. His success was heard by his native Gilead and was asked to return to help fight against the Ammonites. Jephthah agreed but on the condition that in the event of his success against Ammon, he should still remain as there acknowledged head. Jephthah made a vow unto God in Judges 11:31 that he would offer up as a burnt offering whatsoever should come out to meet him if successful. God gave Jephthah victory as the Ammonites were slaughtered but when he returned to mizpeh, his daughter (his only child) came out to meet him with timbrels and dancing. Jephthah was heart-stricken because he remembered his vow to the Lord. His daughter asked that she be allowed to live for two months to prepare for her death, which she was granted. When that time was ended, she returned to her father, who "did with her according to his vow."

Jeremiah – a major prophet of the Old Testament. He was called by God from his mothers' womb and ordained a prophet. Jeremiah teaches all the purpose of the prophet. The purpose of the prophet is to be God's mouthpiece and in doing so will produce results of a rooting out, pulling down, destroying, and a casting down that which has not been sanctioned by the Holy Spirit. The results will also produce within the kingdom a building up and planting. Authority and anointing rested upon Jeremiah and this same type of flow must rest upon prophets of today. Jeremiah denotes a person of purpose, one who was birthed, to serve in the kingdom.

Jeroboam (the sin of) – Jeroboam was the first king of the divided kingdom of Israel that consisted of ten tribes. He was a superintendent under Solomon and was responsible for overseeing the taxes and labors exacted from the tribe of Ephraim. The Lord through Ahijah the prophet told Jeroboam that He would give him ten tribes from the House of David because of Solomon's sin of marrying many wives. Jeroboam eventually became king but became concerned about the Israelites going up to worship in Jerusalem so he devised a plan. He made two golden figures of a sacred calf called Mnevis. He placed one of the figures in Dan and the other in Bethel making them the worship centers. Jereboam devised this plan from his own heart. This is known as the sin of Jereboam. Prophetically the sin of Jeroboam reveals a type of leadership that has insecurity issues and in order to keep the people that type of leader indoctrinates another type of worship that is not of God. That type of change will serve as a hold on the people causing them to not move forward into true worship. This type of worship is created through oppression of leadership.

Jerusalem – The word Jerusalem is divided into two words, Yeru and shalem. Yeru is the Hebrew word that means "the foundation of." The Hebrew word Shalem means "peace." Jerusalem means "The foundation of Peace." Jerusalem was the place where God choose to place His name. (Deut. 12:5)

Jesus – The New Testament is all about the name of the Lord Jesus Christ (Messiah). Jesus is the Name of the Son of God. It should be made clear that Christ and Lord are His titles and are joined together to identify Him as being the one and only "Lord Jesus Christ." Jesus is the author and finisher of our faith, the bishop of our souls, the Apostle and High Priest of our confession. Jesus is also Savior; our most perfect and complete example, He is our Friend. He was the one who was sent from the Father, led captivity captive and gave gifts unto men (Eph. 4:8). He was our sacrifice and the most precious gift.

Jethro – the father in-law of Moses who was able to give him wise counsel. Prophetically, Jethro's are needed for men and women of God in the kingdom. Jethro's are needed in order to give wise council. "For by wise counsel thou shalt make thy war: and in multitude of counsellors there is safety" (Proverbs 24:6).

Jezebel (spirit of) – Jezebel was the daughter of Ethbaal, the king of the Zidonians. She became the influential queen of Israel and the wife of Ahab. She fostered the worship of Canaanite fertility deities, supporting 450 prophets of Baal and 400 prophets of the goddess Ashera (1 Kgs 18:19). Jezebel ruthlessly persecuted the prophets of God causing them to go into hiding. She manufactured the legal death of Naboth the Jezreelite so that her husband could obtain his vineyard (1 Kings 21). In Revelation 2:20, the name of Jezebel was mentioned and used synonymously as a wicked woman. The spirit of Jezebel is a spirit of ungodly unordained teaching within the church. That teaching impregnates any luke warm Christian. It is a teaching of non-submissiveness, a desire to not submit to leadership authority. Whatever is given out or taught by this spirit would be accepted and when accepted can impregnate and cause one to produce whatever it is impregnated by. In Revelation 2:20 the spirit of Jezebel (a teaching spirit) caused them to commit fornication. The spirit of Jezebel despises order, marriage, true worship and apostolic anointing and most importantly the gift of the prophet. (See pornography, soothsayer)

Jochebed – the name Jochebed means, "whose glory is Jehovah." Jochebed was the mother of Moses. She was responsible for placing Moses in a basket placing him in the river. Jochebed prophetically speaks of one who births vision for she birthed Moses.

Joel – a prophet who saw the vision of "the Day of the Lord." He also spoke of the Spirit of the Lord being released in the last days.

John Mark – His Jewish name was John, and his sir name was Mark" (Acts 12:12). He accompanied Paul and Barnabas on their return from Jerusalem to Antioch. In Acts 13:13, when Paul and Barnabas were about to enter upon the more difficult mission John Mark left and returned to Jerusalem to his mother and his home. Barnabas wanted John Mark to accompany him on another journey but Paul refused. However, John Mark was with Paul during Paul's imprisonment at Rome, and he is acknowledged by Paul as one of his few fellow laborers who had been a "comfort" to him during the weary hours of his imprisonment.

John (the Apostle) – the son of Zebedee was called along with this brother James to be one of Jesus' twelve apostles who would accompany him on his ministry. Tradition has it that John lived until at least 100 and passed away in the city of Ephesus. John was present at the resurrection of Jairus' daughter, at Jesus' transfiguration, and at the Garden of Gethsemane before Jesus was arrested. Paul later describes John as a "pillar" of the Jerusalem church. John wrote the fourth (non-synoptic) gospel, three canonical letters, and the book of Revelation.

John (the Baptist) – The cousin of Jesus who was a prophet and forerunner of Jesus. He preached preparing the way of the Lord and did so under an anointing that was reflective of the prophet Elijah.

Joshua – minister who served Moses. Moses then laid hands upon him, which was a divine impartation giving Joshua an anointing and ability to lead the people further. Joshua was the predecessor of Moses. (See Divine impartation).

Jot – (see yod)

Judah - Fourth son of Jacob and father of the tribe of Judah which was one of the twelve tribes of Israel. When his mother Leah gave birth to Judah she said "Now I will praise God." (Genesis 30:35). It was Judah's idea to sell his brother Joseph to a Midianite slave trader rather than leave him to die in the pit (Genesis 37:27). He later became the spokesman for his father Jacob and his brothers when they traveled to Egypt during the famine in Canaan.

Judas Iscariot – One of the original twelve apostles who lost his focus on ministry and allowed satan to enter into him. Judas then betrayed Jesus for thirty pieces of silver (he lost his integrity and was moved by the money). Judas Iscariot prophetically denotes a believer who has lost focus and because of losing that focus creates an opening for the enemy to enter into their mind.

Just – the Hebrew word for just is tsaddiyq (tsad-deek') that means "lawful or righteous. The Greek word for just is dikaios (dik'-ah-yos) which means "right, equitable in character or actions. The word just means to be righteous or right and poses the right character. It denotes one who has been declared innocent, holy or righteous.

Kairos – (see time)

Kaph - the eleventh letter of the Hebrew alphabet, which means, "palm." It denotes the palm of the hand. Kaph is noted in praise, when the kaph (open palm of the hand) is displayed in praise it reveals a request asking the Father to fill that palm with blessing.

Keeper – the Hebrew word ra`ah (raw-aw') which means "to tend and pasture a flock; it generally means to rule. The Father has made His church keepers or stewards who takes care of what God has entrusted to them. (See steward)

Ketubah – Hebrew term for the marriage certificate. Since ancient times the document was not so much used as evidence for marriages but chiefly as a protection of the women's rights.

Ketuvim – Hebrew term that means "writings." (See Writings The)

Keys to the kingdom –Apostolic authority given to the church. This authority allows the church to be able to bind and loose. Keys represent the ability to lock and unlock. (Matt. 16:16-19)

Kiddushin – Hebrew word for sanctification and is used in the Hebrew for entering into Marriage.

Kingdom Anointing - kingdom anointing is a prison breaking yoke destroying anointing that rests within and upon the kingdom of God.

Kingdom Assignment – A portion of God's vision appointed to the believer who is responsible for manifesting on earth that portion of God's vision.

Kingdom of God - The kingdom of God is the Spirit of God living though His people, it is the reign and rule of God on earth through His people. The territory of the kingdom of God is the earth and the heart of the believer. It is through the kingdom that the Hand of God is released that He might exercise His authority on earth.

Kingdom of Heaven – the kingdom of heaven denotes the rules and system in heaven now revealed and followed through on earth.

Kof - the nineteenth letter of the Hebrew alphabet that is equivalent to the English letter "q." Most Lexicons likens the meaning of kof to a hole of an ax for securing the ax head to the handle. Prophetically the letter kof denotes the connection of the body of Christ (His church) to the head of the church who is Christ.

Kohanim – Priests of the Second Temple who were responsible for offering sacrifices at the altar or sanctuary of the Temple; to officiate over sacred functions; and to serve as teachers.

Kohathites – Formed the first of the three divisions of the Levites and were in charge of the most holy portion of the vessels of the tabernacle, including the ark (Num. 4). (See Gershonites, Merarites, Levites)

Kohen Gadol – The Hebrew term meaning "High Priest." (See High Priest)

Laban – the brother of Rebekah and father of Leah and Rachel. Jacob resided with Laban for twenty years in Paddan-aram and married two of Laban's daughters Rachel and Leah. Jewish tradition labels Laban as a symbol of deceit due to his attempts to exploit and cheat Jacob.

Labour – is denoted as a human hand, or strength in Scripture. Prophetically speaking labour denotes one who works in the kingdom through much toil and adversity.

Lamed - the twelfth letter of the Hebrew alphabet that is equivalent to the English letter "L." The word lamed means a yoke for oxen.

Laodicea – Laodicea was the seventh of the seven churches mentioned in Revelation chapter three. It was 45 miles Southeast from Philadelphia. It was a fortified city which sat on seven hills, which were drained by two brooks. In AD 61 there was an earthquake and the city of Laodicea suffered a great loss but it restored itself without requiring aid from Nero. The Laodiceans were a self-sufficient people. Medicine, production of eyesalve, wool distribution, manufacturing and banking brought fame to Laodicea. Christ has no commendation to this church but much is complained. Paul speaks of a problem with this church in Colossians 2:1. This was a self-centered church that boasted of themselves and of their goods. Their satisfaction was based on their physical accomplishments and status not their walk with God. Christ was not the focal point of the church at Laodicea. What the church at Laodicea failed to realize was their position as far as Christ was concerned. They couldn't see it because their prosperity and ego had blinded them. Christ saw them for what they really were. He saw them as wretched, miserable, poor, blind and naked. Laodicea was a luke warm group of people who could care less about Jesus Christ's claim on their lives or upon them as a church. It made Jesus Christ sick to his stomach. He said "you are neither hot nor cold, if you open the door and let me in, I will sup with you. If you repent, you will sit with me on my throne and you will reign with me." (See Philadelphia, Sardis, Thyatira, Smyrna, Pergamos, Ephesus)

Latter Rain – a rain for harvest. This is type rain denotes a word for a season, a word that will nurture that which was previously planted and produce a kingdom harvest. Both the former and latter rain denotes a season and time for planting and harvesting. This type of rain prophetically speaking is called a kingdom rain. (See former rain)

Law - The first five books of the Old Testament. The Law is also referred to as the "Torah." The term Torah means "Teachings or instruction" and is derived from the root word yarah (yaw-raw'), which means, "to shoot (an arrow)" intending to "hit the mark." These books are also called "the Five Books of Moses" or the "Pentateuch." Prophetically the law (torah) speaks of the Word of God that hits the mark or meets the need of the believer. (See the Pentateuch)

Laying on of hands – It was a symbol of blessing. In Genesis 48:14-20 Jacob laid hands on his grandsons Ephraim and Manasseh and blessed them. The laying on of hands is also identified with ordination. Paul ordained Timothy to the ministry through the laying on of my hands (1 Tim. 1:6). The laying on of hands denotes one commissioning someone into apostolic work. (See Commission, ordination)

Leaven – Leaven prophetically denotes false teaching that is able to spread. (1 Cor. 5:6-7). In the Old Testament, the Jews were required to remove all leaven from their homes and to only eat unleavened bread. Unleavened bread denotes uncompromised Word.

Legalism – mans attempt to create rules and regulations in order to indoctrinate believers. It is when rules have preempted faith and grace.

Levi – the third son of Jacob and father of the tribe of Levi called the Levites.

Levites - The Levites were the ministering persons of the Sanctuary. While Israel was sojourning through the wilderness, it was the job of the Levites to carry the tabernacle, disband the tabernacle, transport the tabernacle and set it up. They were also to conduct worship at the tent where God dwelt. Aaron and his descendants became priest. The Levites did not acquire territory of their own but were assigned a number of cities in the territories of the other tribes. In temple times especially the period of the Second temple, the Levites were the singers, chanting the chorus during the services. The Levites were divided into three sections. (See Kohathites, Gershonites, Merarites)

Lion of the Tribe of Judah – The name of the Lord Jesus Christ that depicts His sovereignty, power and authority. This name also depicts His lineage from the tribe of Judah as a descendent of King David.

Locust – the Hebrew word 'arbeh (ar-beh') refers to a grasshopper. The root word is rabah (raw-baw'), which means, "to increase" A Locust is a grasshopper type animal that increases or grows rapidly, it moves around by leaping. Prophetically speaking, the locust denotes a leaping fast growing belief allowed without being tested.

Locust (spirit of) - The spirit of locusts is a fast growing and fast moving spirit that attempts to grow and sneak past the prophetic apostolic gifts functioning in the Kingdom. It is untested unbiblical truth which attempts to rapidly become doctrine. This spirit appears popular to those who lack biblical balance and direction of the Holy Spirit. Many beliefs coming forth today have not been tested or tried by scripture but because of its popularity it has leaped and increased rapidly.

Lodebar - means "place of no pasture" or "place of no life." Lodebar was where the son of Jonathan lived named Methphibosheth. (see Methphibosheth)

Longsuffering – the ability to bear and endure a season of hardship inconvenience and wrongdoing and bear with that patiently and tolerantly.

Lust – a desired craving and longing for that which is forbidden.

Man – male who is one of great strength and authority that prevails as a warrior, a leader and strength in the home.

Manasseh – The son of Joseph and grandson of Jacob. Manasseh was also one of the twelve tribes of Israel. Jacob blessed Joseph's two sons Ephraim and Manasseh. The younger (Ephraim) would take precedence over his brother Manasseh.

Manna – Food from heaven. The Manna fell during the night upon the dew and the Israelites were instructed by Moses to gather each morning one omer (approximately 4 quarts) and a double portion on the sixth day for the Sabbath. The Bible derives the name Manna from the question "man hu?" Man hu was what the Israelites asked when they saw Manna for the first time. Prophetically speaking Manna denotes a fresh word given by the Holy Spirit it is the believers' daily bread which Jesus prayed for in Matthew chapter six.

Mantle – a cloak worn by prophets symbolizing their office and anointing. Prophetically those who walk in apostolic anointing wear a mantle placed upon them by the Holy Spirit.

Marketplace – Marketplace is from the Greek word kategoros, which is made up of two words, kata which means down and agora which means Town Square or marketplace. The marketplace is the place where the enemy attempts to place one on public display in order to produce humiliation in the heart and mind. The marketplace is where Jesus has purchased the believer. (See redeeming)

Marror – a bitter herb that was served at the Passover Seder. Marror served as a reminder of the bitter slavery experience and suffering of the Israelites while in Egypt. It also served as part of the covenant meal served on the night Jesus was betrayed. Jesus said in Matthew 26:23, "He that dippeth his hand with me in the dish, the same shall betray me." The one that dipped his hand in the dish along with Jesus was his covenant brother. The meaning was that as brothers they stood together and to never forget their history; it meant that they celebrated and commemorated this time of Passover to rekindle the brotherly relationship between the Hebrew people. Yet it was the one who ate the marror with Jesus who would betray him. (See Seder)

Masterbuilder - comes from the Greek word architekton (ar-khee-tek'-tone) from which we get the English word "architect." Paul was a head builder, masterbuilder, contractor, or director of works in the kingdom of God. A Masterbuilder is the spirit of an Apostle.

Meal (grain) Offering - called the minchah in Hebrew (Lev. 2:1). This offering is a sweet-savor offering prepared from the ingredients of grain, flour and oil. The flour was not fine flour but a type called solet which was meal made from the hard kernels of wheat. The solet could contain no lumps. The type of oil used was olive oil. Animal sacrifices were accompanied by mandatory meal offerings. The sacrifice was also seasoned with salt. Frankincense was placed on top just before the offering was brought to the altar. This offering denotes the person and character of Christ who was a sweet savour. The Solet consisted of no lumps which speak of Jesus who displayed no lumps or unevenness in His humanity. The oil used represents the Holy Spirit. The salt added denotes the incorruptibleness of the Savior, frankincense poured on top of the offering denotes the spirit of praise that covers all that is being offered.

Mem - the thirteenth letter of the Hebrew alphabet that is equivalent to the English letter "m." The meaning of this word is water and prophetically speaking, Mem denotes the Holy Spirit.

Merarites – an order of the priesthood responsible for carrying the heavier portions of the tabernacle mainly, the boards, bars, sockets, and pillars. (See Gershonites, Kohathites, Levites)

Methphibosheth – The son of Jonathan who was crippled at an early age. He felt very low of himself referring to himself as a dog and he lived in a placed called Lodebar, which means "a place of no pasture or place of no life." Methphibosheth denotes a type of individual who possessed the possibility of greatness but lost that opportunity because of a fall and because of the fall feels low of themselves; their fall has crippled their outlook on life. (See Lodebar)

Molechism - The name Molech means "king" and was the idol god of the Ammonites. The statue was of brass and it sat on a brass throne. This deity had the head of a calf that adorned a crown; its arms were extended as a sign to embrace all those who approached it. Worshippers of this idol dedicated their children to it. They would burn a fire under the idol causing the figure to become hot and then the infants were either shaken or passed through the flames and ignited arms of this idol which was to serve as favor to this deity. Molechism is the practice of giving up your seed in order to appease someone else (another god). Molechism also denotes the spirit of abortion.

Moriah – the mountain where the Akedah took place. Moriah was also the mountain where God appeared unto David in the threshing floor of Ornan the Jebusite. Solomon eventually leveled this mountain and built the Holy Temple. Prophetically speaking Mt Moriah is called the place. The place in the Hebrew is called the *maqowm* which speaks of the exalted place, the third dimension, the place were full maturity is exhibited through the believer. (See Akedah, threshing floor)

Moses – the most authoritative figure in the Old Testament. Moses was a leader sent by God to lead the Israelites out of the bondage of Egypt. He was not only a leader but also a deliverer, prophet, a lawgiver, counselor, pioneer, mentor and a scribe. Moses denotes an apostle in its truest form.

Mother (Spiritual) - The Hebrew word for mother means the bond or glue of the family and home. A spiritual Mother is one who is able to bring together or bind together order within the local ministry and body of Christ. A spiritual mother wars in the spirit against the enemy who attempts to loosen the family both in the home and local ministry. Spiritual mothers are always great women of prayer and it is through that life of prayer the spiritual mother is able to keep things together.

Mouth (of Praise) – The New Testament word for mouth denotes a gash in the face, an opening as the opening of the earth. The opening also speaks of that of a canal or river whereas a river flows out of that opening. A mouth of praise is the opening of your spirit, which allows the praises of God to flow out.

Muzzling the ox – a term used to describe holding back finances from those ministries that have labored. (1 Tim. 5:18)

Mysteries – the hidden things concealed in the mind of God that are revealed to the believer through the Holy Spirit.

Naphtali – One of the twelve sons of Jacob and father of the tribe Naphtali.

Naphtali (tribe) – One of the tribes of Israel. The men of the tribe of Naphtali were known as courageous warriors. Prophetically speaking the tribe of Naphtali denotes men who are the heads of their homes. They serve as leaders, worshippers and most importantly courageous warriors in the spirit.

Nation (great) – In Genesis 12:2 the Father told Abraham that he would make of him a "great nation." The word great in the Lexicon is described as a cord that is twisted together which denotes strength. The word for great in the Hebrew means magnificent. The word nation is the Hebrew word *gowy* (go'ee) which comes from the Hebrew root word *gevah* which means "a human back." The word nation denotes a body. God told Abraham that out of him would come a magnificent body or a magnificent mass of people making up one magnificent nation.

Nehemiah - The name Nehemiah means consolation of the Lord. Nehemiah was a cupbearer of King Artaxerxes Longimanus. Certain Jews arrived from Judea and gave Nehemiah a deplorable account of the state of Jerusalem. Nehemiah's assignment was to rebuild the walls of Jerusalem and to restore the city to its former state and dignity. In doing this Nehemiah reestablished order that was either forgotten or neglected. Prophetically speaking, Nehemiah denotes the gift of apostleship. He was a builder and a restorer. While building the wall, he charged the people to hold a sword in one hand and building equipment in the other. This denotes a type of balance the people had to walk in while operating under the authority of Nehemiah. Nehemiah also because of his charge received favor from the King.

Nehushtan – the name of the brazen serpent made by Moses while the Children of Israel were in the wilderness. This same serpent was continuously worshipped from the time of Moses until the time of king Hezekiah of Judah. It was King Hezekiah who finally destroyed the image. Nehushtan reveals how one can worship a dead thing or a dead issue not realizing that the dead thing had been done away with.

New Birth – a transformation by which the Holy Spirit baptizes and individual into the kingdom of God. The old man has become new

New Covenant – The new covenant is spoken about first in the book of Jeremiah. The New covenant is the fulfillment of all previous covenants. In that fulfillment it abolishes the old temporal elements of the old previous covenants and brings the believer into the position of being a recipient of all that God has promised in the New Covenant. The New covenant is a covenant in which Jesus purchased through his death on the cross. It is the covenant written the hearts of the people of God.

New Creation – those who were born again through the new birth by accepting Jesus Christ as their personal savior. A new creation is an adopted daughter and son that were born into the family of God.

New Wine – In Matthew 9:17 it reads "Neither do men put new wine into old bottles: else the bottles break, and the wine runneth out, and the bottles perish: but they put new wine into new bottles, and both are preserved". The new wine is the refreshing of the Holy Spirit that is to dwell in the rejuvenated believer; the one who has been baptized into a higher realm in God. A new wine represents a new flow of God, which brings about purpose. (See wineskin)

Nimrod – the name Nimrod means "rebellion or we will revolt." He was a descendant of Cush and established the first imperial kingdom, which was an empire in Shinar known as Babylonia. Nimrod gradually enlarged his kingdoms. He was known as the "the mighty one in the earth" however, scholars have referred to him as "trapper or hunter of men and a tyrant. Nimrod denotes an oppressor who uses brute force to accomplish and obtain self-proclaimed goals. This is seen in many leaders and pastors who lack godly confidence.

Noah – a preacher of righteousness, builder of the Ark. Noah's spirit denotes one who walks in apostolic anointing. He was charged to build something that had never been done before in the midst of non-believers. He built the Ark, which prophetically speaks of a place of refuge and restoration.

Noah's Ark - Noah was instructed by the Lord to build an Ark. Noah was given the specifics as to what the Father wanted. God's instructions to Noah mention the type of wood to be used; the ark had to consist of rooms, and that the ark was to be pitched within and without. The word room is the Hebrew word qen (kane) which speaks of a nest, chamber or dwelling. The rooms were to be places of dwelling that were to be occupied. The rooms in the ark prophetically speak of a place for someone to come and rest, to be covered and restored. The rooms in the ark represent the local church and the position that it takes concerning the lost which is that individuals are to come, be covered, and be restored into their rightful place within the kingdom. The ark was to be pitched within and without. The Hebrew word for pitch is kopher (ko'-fer) which means "to properly cover" with a literal meaning as "to cover a village." The rooms in the ark were to be nests that were to be covered. The nests denote complete covering whereby they would not be exposed. The covering serves as protection, for the local church is to cover and protect those who come in. The word for Ark is the Hebrew word tebah (tay-baw'), which means "a box." Another translation refers to the Ark as a basket. The tebah consisted of a huge square box with a flat bottom. It had no sails, no rudder and no other mechanisms that would allow the ark to be driven or steered. The box represents the church; the rooms inside are the protective rooms within the ministry, and the protective rooms serve as a safe haven. The Ark had a space (18 in. by 18 in.) for window space (so that the light could come in). That space was in the third loft (third realm). The window kept all looking upward and not downward (Psalms 24:7-10). Looking upward represents the King of Glory in the midst of His people. Jesus is the center and head of every ministry. As long as He is the object of everyone's desire and worship, the ministry will continue to move. Noah's Ark prophetically denotes the local church becoming a safe haven for the lost, the wounded, the dying. It is where they are nursed back to health, covered in the spirit, covered in prayer and then repositioned in the kingdom.

Nun - the fourteenth letter of the Hebrew alphabet which means "fish." The Greek word for fish is ichthus, which is an acronym for the following Greek words: Iesus Christos Theou Uios Soter, meaning "Jesus (the) Messiah, God's Son, Savior."

Oath – The Greek word is horkos (hor'-kos), which is a fence or a sacred restraint placed on oneself. It is the giving of a person's word that binds that person to fulfilling that Word. In Hebrews 6:17 God confirmed the promise of His immutability by an oath. In other words the Father restrained Himself from going back on His word. (See immutability)

Occult - the word occult comes from the Latin word occultus, which means "hidden," or "secrets." The operation of the occult is demonic in nature as it attempts to grant unlawful access to powers and forces of an ungodly and demonic nature. The occult includes all forms of witchcraft and is in violation of the first commandment.

Occultic – the practice of the occult

Offerings (Old Testament) - There are two types of offerings specified in the book of Leviticus, the sweet-savour offerings and the nonsweet-savour offerings. The sweet-savour offerings demonstrated that the sacrifice was acceptable to God. The sweet savour offerings were the burnt, meal and peace offerings. The nonsweet-savour offering demonstrated that the sinner was unacceptable however, God's justice fell upon the sacrifice and it became the sinners substitute. The sweet-savour offerings were voluntary and the nonsweet-savour offerings were mandatory. (See the burnt offering, meat (grain) offering, peace offering, sin offering, trespass offering, wave or heave offering)

Omri – the King of Israel, father of Ahab. Until the reign of Ahab, Omri was known as the worse king to ever sit on the throne of Israel.

One - The Hebrew word for one is 'echad (ekh-awd') which means once or once and for all. The number one also denotes divine unity, supremacy and independency, suffiency that needs no other. The number one reveals the unity of God

Oppression – The state of a spirit –filled believer being weighed down superficially by an unclean spirit. This type of oppression usually occurs when disobedience is involved. A believer can step into a situation that is ungodly and the individual not being spirit lead may have fallen into a state of the flesh and the results of that has caused the believer to be both guilty and feel that guilt. The guilt will lead to unforgivenss of themselves, which in turn will lead to oppression.

Oral Gifts – gifts of Prophecy, diverse tongues, interpretation of tongues (1 Cor. 12:8-10)

Ordain - to ordain means to place in order. To ordain someone means to place someone in an order that God has sanctioned. This order pertains to ministry, birthing, fathering and then apostolically releasing. The laying on of hands does ordaining. (See laying on of hands)

Outer Court - The outer court is the first room of the tabernacle of Moses. It also represents the first dimension or the first level of maturity.

Overcome – The word overcome is the Greek word nikao (nik-ah'-o), which means success through conquering, it also means to prevail or get the victory. Believers are overcomers through Jesus Christ who has given His Church the victory and caused them to triumph.

Passover (Feast) - The Feast of the Passover commemorated the final plague in Egypt when the firstborn of the Egyptians died and the Israelites were spared because they took the blood of a lamb and smeared it on the their doorposts (Ex. 12:11, 21, 27, 43, 48). This was an annual feast which is to take place on the 14th day of the first month. The Feast of the Passover speaks of Christ, our Deliverer. (See unleavened bread, firstfruits)

Patibulum – the crossbeam that a victim who was being crucified had to carry. The patibulum weighed between 50 and 100 pounds across his shoulders. The victim's arms were extended and the crossbeams were tied so that the crossbeam would not fall of or be thrown by the victim. (See Stipe)

Pe - the seventeenth letter of the Hebrew alphabet which means "blowing with the mouth" literally or figuratively. Pe denotes the breath of God giving life to His people. The breath of God is the Holy Spirit of God.

Peace – The word peace is usually associated with an English word to mean no war or absence of strife however this does not adequately describe the word peace. The Hebrew word for peace is shalom and is derived from the verbal root word shalam which means, "To pay" in the context of restoring or replacing something. The verb shalem literally means to make whole. When one bestows peace to someone it means you wish them to be of good health and to be whole. The Peace of God consists of being in Good health and being whole or complete.

Peace Offering - It is called Zevach Shelamim in the Hebrew (Lev. 3:1). It means "a sacrifice of well being." The meaning is "a gift to appease some-one who has been offended-and such was not the intent." Others have connected the word with another meaning to repay, make good with reference to a payment of a vow. Christ became the Zevach Shelamim or peace offering. This sacrifice presents a picture of reconciliation, making possible communion with God.

Peculiar People – the possession of people who are over and above all others. This possession belongs to God (1 Pet. 2:9)

Pentateuch - The word Pentateuch is made up of two Greek words the first being penta which means five and teuchoi which means "books." As early as the 1st century, these five books were written on one long scroll signaling that they are one unit.

Pentecost (Feast of) - The second annual Feast also called the Feast of Weeks. Pentecost is the New Testament Greek name which means "fiftieth." This Feast began on the fiftieth day after the Passover Sabbath. This Feast was separate from the Feast of the Passover and the Feast of Tabernacles; it stood alone. There was a span of about four months between this Feast and the Feast of Tabernacles (Day of Trumpets), which represents a waiting period. In Acts 1:3; Jesus showed Himself 40 days after He was crucified. In Acts 2:1, on the Day of Pentecost, which began on the 50th day, the Holy Spirit was released into waiting disciples. The Feast of Pentecost represents a Holy Ghost experience. It was an experience that initiated the forming of the church, the Ekklesia (the called-out ones). (See Passover, unleavened bread, firstfruits, Pentecost, day of the trumpet, Day of Atonement, feast of Tabernacles)

Perfected Praise - katartizo (kat-ar-tid'-zo), the verb means to mend nets. This word actually means to adjust, to articulate, to mend if needed. The perfected praises are those who at one time have been broken but the Father has mended them back together. Those who have been mended back together and understand the importance of where God has brought them from are His "Perfected Praise."

Pergamos (the Church) – Pergamos was the third of the seven churches mentioned in the book of Revelation chapter two. Pergamos was inland and about 60 miles north of Smyrna. There in Pergamos was a 200,000-volume library and a temple of the god Aesculapius which was referred to as the Roman god of healing. Upon the highest hill stood the altar of Zeus. The statue of Zeus along with the statue of Aesculapius stood approximately 800 feet high and could plainly be called the seat of Satan. Pergamos had little or no commerce but was remarkable for its institution of learning. It was a city of refinement and science especially medicine. It was in Pergamos that the act of curing skins for writing was perfected. The word parchment was derived from the process of curing skins to be used for writing. Ephesus and Smyrna were wicked cities of idolatry but Pergamos was worse, it was known as Satan's throne. In the temple of Aesculapius was the wreathed serpent and behind this serpent was Satan. This idol was used in ceremonies of healing and was substituted for the Lord Jesus Christ. The Roman government severely persecuted the church at Pergamos and Jesus Christ commends them for standing up to that persecution but He said, I have something against you, because you've allowed the Balaamites to come in to lead you into ways of immorality and idol worship. You have allowed yourselves to compromise, confuse my name, my new birth, my healing power, gifts of the Spirit, my holiness, my concern and compassion for suffering people, my love and followed after the things of the world but if you repent, "I will give you a new name." (See Laodicea, Philadelphia, Sardis, Thyatira, Smyrna, Ephesus)

Philadelphia (the church) – Philadelphia was the sixth of the seven churches mentioned in the book of Revelation chapter three. It was 25 miles South of Sardis and named for its founder Attalus Philadelphis, who was King of Pergamos. The word Philadelphia means brotherly love. Today the city is named Allah Sehir, meaning City of God and is largely populated by Greeks. Philadelphia was a small struggling church however; they kept His word and did not deny the name of Christ. Philadelphia is the second of the seven churches that was not rebuked or reproved, the other was Smyrna. The differences in the two were Philadelphia was small but faithful and Smyrna was persecuted and it suffered. Jesus didn't have a real problem with this church. Christ said "I will keep you in the hour of temptation." (See Laodicea, Sardis, Thyatira, Smyrna, Pergamos, Ephesus)

Pneumatology – the Old Testament word for the spirit is ruwach (roo'-akh), which means "spirit or wind resembling breath." In the New Testament, the word used for Spirit is Pneuma (pnyoo'-mah) which means "the breath of God, the Wind of God, the Holy Spirit, or the Spirit of Christ." Pneumatology is the study of the Holy Spirit. Prophetically speaking Pneumatology denotes the study of the moving of the Holy Spirit within the Body of Christ.

Pomegranates and Bells (High Priest Garments) - At the hem of the robe of the high priest were small pomegranates of blue, purple, and scarlet, along with golden bells. According to tradition, there were 72 bells and pomegranates with ends of gold. The pomegranate is a fruit that possesses many seeds. The multi-seeded pomegranate at the hem of the robe reveals the ability to produce, create and bring about purpose within the kingdom. The pomegranate represents the spirit of vision. The gold bells reveal life, for as long as the priest functioned within the garments and the bells were heard, it meant the priest was still alive and functioning. If the bells stopped ringing it meant that the priest was dead. The pomegranates depicted at the hem of the robe depict the spirit of vision and the bells reveal the life of that vision.

Pornography - Pornography is the deception of an erotic behavior designed primarily to cause sexual excitement. Pornography is also a spirit that produces an erotic behavior that gives false gratification.

Potential – a possibility that allows one to become who or what God has ordained them to be.

Power Gifts – Gift of Faith, working of Miracles, Gifts of healing (1 Cor. 12:8-10)

Prayer – a petition to God coming from the sincere heart. It is the heart felt desire of the believer. Prayer is also the communication and fellowship of the believer with God.

Prayer Shawl – a garment worn by priest. The prayer shawl was also called the Tallith. The tallith was a square outer garment which consisted of fringes that were affixed to every corner; those fringes were called tzitzits. The fringes were to remind the wearer of the Lords commandments listed in Numbers 15:37-41. Tzitzit is also called (gedil), were intertwined threads or twisted work that were wrapped or knotted. Prophetically, the prayer shawl teaches how the priests of God must be covered in prayer.

Predecessor – a spiritual son or daughter anointed to lead and take vision further. A predecessor must receive a divine impartation from their spiritual father.

Pride – to be inflated with self-conceit or high-minded.

Principalities – high or chief ranking spirits that rule over territories and regions. Principalities are ruling spirits who have dominion.

Process - a continuing development involving many changes. Process is necessary for those who are called into kingdom work and responsibility.

Promotion - Promotion is the exaltation that comes from God. "For promotion cometh neither from the east, nor from the west, nor from the south. But God is the judge: he putteth down one, and setteth up another." (Psalm 75:6-7).

Prophecy – the voice of God's thoughts, mind and will from heaven to earth. It brings unseen creations into their physical existence on earth.

Prophesy – To foretell events, divinely speak under the inspiration of the Holy Ghost.

Prophet – One who speaks under the unction of the Holy Ghost. Prophets function along with the apostolic company, the five-fold ministry. The Father speaks a Word outside of time in eternity and that word must get into the earth; the prophet is that vessel of God that God uses to get that word out of eternity into time. Time then must catch up to the prophetic word. Prophets are utilized by God in order to get a word from eternity into the Earth realm.

Prophets (the) – the second division of the Old Testament Hebrew Bible. The Books of the Prophets were composed of the Former Prophets, which are the books of Joshua, Judges, Samuel and Kings and of the latter Prophets, which are composed of Isaiah, Jeremiah, Ezekiel, and the Twelve.

Prostitute (Temple) – Temple prostitutes were persons employed by the temple to perform sexual intercourse. A spirit of a temple prostitute denotes one who partakes in evil for a fee in order to appease someone or something. The mindset of this practice is that sexual favors constitute religious offerings. Such a practice empowers the spirit of belialism (see Belial spirit of).

Prudent – one who uses good judgment in handling practical matters. Prophetically speaking a prudent person is a believer who uses sound wisdom and judgment in handling matters concerning their personal lives and the kingdom

Purpose - the kingdom-oriented charge from God to you, which will cause you to affect not only the kingdom but also the world. Purpose is the believers' reason for existence within the kingdom.

Quails – In Numbers 11:31 the Lord sent a wind which caused the quails to come around the camp of Israel. When they landed the amount of quails numbered 3 feet and 8 inches high so that they could be caught and killed. The quail denotes a provision for the Israelites provided by God while they went through their time of transition.

Quarantania – It was a mountain which stood approximately 1200 feet high and about 7 miles north-west of Jericho. It is believed that Quarantania was the exceedingly high mountain Jesus was taken to where satan shewed Him all the kingdoms of the world and the glory of them during the time of the temptation of Jesus in Matthew 4:8.

Quaternion – a band of four soldiers who guarded Peter while he was in custody. One quaternion has the responsibility for the watch of the night. (Acts 12:4)

Queen of heaven – the word queen is the Hebrew word malkah that means, "Worship" or "goddess." Queen of heaven was an idol that included worship that the Jews migrated to. The word queen also denotes royalty in a female form and was used for the wives of Solomon who were of a royal race. They were warned in the book of Jeremiah however the people responded that they vowed to worship in this order. The Queen of heaven is seen in many areas of religious worship.

Quicken – to be made alive spiritually.

Quicksand – there was a place north of the coast of Africa that was known for its places of quicksand. This place was called the Syrtis Major or "Great bay." When Paul was shipwrecked in Acts chapter 27 they were to be careful of the quicksands. Prophetically quicksand denotes dangerous traps set by the enemy that will devour the believer if the believer is not prayerfully watchful.

Quiver – a quiver is a sheath (pouch) for arrows. The quiver suspended from the shoulder. A quiver is a pouch that houses artillery. Prophetically a quiver denotes the Word of God.

Rabshakeh (the spirit) – Rabshakeh was a messenger sent by King Sennacherib to taunt and intimidate Hezekiah. Sennacherib, King of Assyria was getting ready to conquer Jerusalem and he sent his man Rabshakeh to intimidate the inhabitants of Jerusalem. As the people planned to withstand the siege Rabshakeh told them they did not have a chance, that they were going to try and run but there is no one that would be able to help them because the Assyrian Army was the greatest army in the world. Rabshakeh goes on to state that if the people of Jerusalem give in, they will send them to a place where they could relax. The Assyrian Army wanted the land that belonged to the believers. King Hezekiah prayed and the Lord then sent the prophet Isaiah who assured Hezekiah that the Assyrians would not take the city; they would not even shoot one arrow. The spirit of Rabshakeh denotes a spirit of intimidation towards the people of God

Rahab - A woman of Jericho who received the spies sent by Joshua to spy out the land. She hid them in her house from the pursuit of her countrymen and because of her kindness she was saved with all her family when the Israelites took the city. She eventually became the wife of Salmon and the ancestress of the Messiah. Rahab denotes one who showed favor to the men of God and in turn God blessed her and her house

Ram Skins – A covering noted in the Tabernacle of Moses. This covering was dyed red. Red speaks of sacrifice. The ram also represents sacrifice. According to Exodus 29:15-21, Aaron and his sons, who represents the pastor along with those in leadership, were to take part in the sacrificing of the ram, whose blood was to be sprinkled around the altar. The blood from the ram was also to be placed upon the tip of the right ear, which speaks of the sacrificing of the head in leadership. It means that head knowledge will not get in the way of knowledge that flows from the Holy Spirit. The blood of the ram was also sprinkled on the right thumb of Aaron and his sons. This sprinkling typifies the submitting to authority and the coming into alignment with order. It means that the hands are sacrificed and will devote time to the working of the ministry. Blood from the ram was then placed upon the great right toe, typifying the sacrificing of the feet that will cause the headship of the house to constantly walk in the direction of God's voice. Blood was also sprinkled on the garments of the priests, which typifies total sacrifice of persons as they are submitted to kingdom work. The dyed ram skins covering reveals to us the prayer of consecration that must be done within leadership. It is a prayer that will keep all eyes in focus on what God intends within the ministry. There must be constant sacrificing of the head, the hands, and the feet. This is a prayer of covering that takes place in the leadership ministry. As the ram was an offering, so are the ministers' (Aaron and his sons') offerings. Romans 12:1 instruct us to present our bodies a living sacrifice, blameless and well pleasing unto God. This is the attitude of the servant within the house: that all the ministers are servants who have sacrificed themselves unto the service of the Lord. All being in unity will be a blameless, well-pleasing offering unto the Lord. Through the sacrificing of ministers, the house would, in turn, be blessed. The covering of the ram's skins represents the prayer and spirit of sacrifice. (see goats hair, badgers skin)

Rape – to take something by force violently without permission. The end thereof is the victim feeling worthless, degrading and lacks confidence. (See Shechem the spirit)

Rebekah – the wife of Isaac and mother of Esau and Jacob. Rebekah helped Jacob to obtain the blessing of Isaac. Rebekah denotes one who assists one in getting to their destiny.

Redeeming – The Greek word exagorazo (ex-ag-or-ad'-zo). This word is made up of two words. Ek (ek) which means to be removed, the second word is agorazo (ag-or-ad'-zo) which means "marketplace). Exagorazo means, "To be removed from the market place never to be resold again." Jesus was our exagorazo; He removed us from the guilty public display at the marketplace never to be resold again.

Rehashing (spiritual) – a rehearsing of continuous unsuccessful events within ministry leaving no room for or expecting any change. The same results of failure have become the expected and normal means of functioning.

Repentance - The Hebrew word for repentance is shuwb (shoob). It means "to turn back (hence, away) to turn again; to retreat." This word shuwb expresses the thought of turning or returning. The Greek word for repentance is metanoeo (met-an-o-eh'-o). It is made up of two words. The first word is meta (met-ah'), which means "after," implying change; the second word is noieo (noy-eh'-o), which means "to perceive, exercise the mind, observe, comprehend, heed." Metanoeo means "a change of mind."

Resh - the twentieth letter of the Hebrew alphabet that is equivalent to the English letter "r." This word denotes something as being the head meaning first in place, time or rank. Prophetically speaking, the letter resh denotes Jesus who is the head of the believer's life, the head of the church.

Resurrection – to be raised from the dead and brought back to life.

Resurrection Power – the power of God in demonstration which will in turn bring back from the dead someone or something. Resurrection power prophetically speaks of restoration to those who have suffered great loss.

Reuben – the first son of Jacob and father of the tribe of Reuben. Reuben was the brother who pleaded with his brothers not to kill Joseph but to cast him into a pit instead. Reuben lost the privileges that traditionally were given to first-born sons because he had an affair with Bilhah, who was Jacobs's concubine. Jacob prophesied to Rueben that he was unstable as water, he would not excel because he went into his fathers bed and defiled it.

Revelation – the unveiling of truth which is the true intended interpretation of the Spirit.

Revelation Gifts - Word of wisdom, word of knowledge, discerning of spirits (1 Cor. 12:8-10)

Robe of the ephod – the robe of the ephod was dark blue and descended to the knees. It was like the robe that Christ wore that the soldiers cast lost for. It was a seamless garment that was made with a woven, edge-like collar around it so that it would not tear. It represents the bestowing of the spirit and anointing of grace.

Rosh – Hebrew word that means "head of" or "the beginning of."

Rosh Hashanah – The Hebrew term meaning "the beginning or head of the Year." It is the Jewish New Year celebrated on the first and second days of the month of Tishre (September-October).

Rosh Hodesh – the Hebrew term meaning the beginning or head of a month.

Ruth – was a female born in Moab. She became the daughter in-law of Naomi through marriage. When her husband died Ruth agreed to stay with her mother in-law Naomi and both Ruth and Naomi eventually moved to Bethlehem where Ruth would meet her husband a rich man named Boaz. Boaz loved Ruth and eventually both Ruth and Boaz was blessed with a child named Obed. Obed became the father of Jessie. Jessie became the father of King David. Messiah would eventually come through the lineage of David. Ruth was the great-grand mother of King David and the ancestor to the Messiah Jesus the Christ.

Salt Covenant – When two parties were making an agreement, once the terms of a covenant had been agreed upon, each party would put a small pinch of salt in the others pouch. This signified that the covenant could only be broken if the exact grains of salt were returned to the original owner. (God made several of these with the Israelites Lev. 2:13; Num. 18:19; 2 Chr. 13:5). Salt is a time proven and consistent preservative, that prevents decay and corruption. The Salt covenant is eternal, enduring, purifying, never changing, and abiding forever; it is the very symbol of God's character and reliability. And the term "Covenant of Salt," is indicative of the everlasting nature of the Covenant relationship between God and his Children.

Samech - the fifteenth letter of the Hebrew alphabet that denotes a symbol of support, protection, and memory.

Sanctify – the Hebrew word for sanctify is qadash (kaw-dash') which means to be clean both ceremoniously and morally. It also means to appoint. When one is sanctified God has cleansed them and appointed them.

Sardis (the church) – Sardis was the fifth of the seven churches mentioned in Revelation chapter three. Sardis was about 27 or 28 miles South of Thyatira. The city was wealthy and filled with pride. In Revelation 3:1, the speaker is identified as He that hath the seven Spirits of God. The seven Spirits of God is a phrase used to show of the completeness, the fullness and diversified actions and ministries of the Holy Spirit. Not only are the "the seven Spirits of God" mentioned but the seven stars are also noted. The stars are the lightbearers (leaders) of the local assembly and their responsibility is to shine for Christ, to reflect the light of Christ and of Heaven to people who are in darkness. Christ has the seven Spirits and the seven stars. Sardis had the name that they were alive but God knew the church at Sardis was dead. It was a "formalistic church," a church given over to formal or ritualistic worship. It had a form of Godliness but denying the power. The name Sardis means "the escaping one," or those who "come out." Christ warns Sardis to be alert and strengthen those things that remain committed. Those who will give their lives needed to be strengthened. Christ admonishes them to remember, hold fast and repent. Evidently there was a message that was preached within this church because Christ reminds them to keep in mind what they heard, and hold to it in their hearts and repent. (See Laodicea, Philadelphia, Thyatira, Smyrna, Pergamos, Ephesus, seven Spirits of God)

Scepter - The Hebrew word is shebet (shay'-bet). This particular word denotes a branch that has been taken or cut from a branch, or to branch off. This particular branch that brook off from a branch denotes authority that was broken off and given. The branch or stick known as the sceptre is the authority given to a particular leader from the authority of the Father. The sceptre is used for warding off any animals that would attempt to harm the sheep. This is the authority of Apostles, Prophets and others who walk in apostolic anointing.

Scribe – Scribes are Prophets who serve as the fingers of the Holy Spirit. They seek the Lord, do the Law, and teach the Law. They write as the Holy Spirit speaks, and those words are inscribed on the walls of the Hearts of the people (Heb. 8:10). (See Ezra)

Seder – the word Seder literally means order and it was the ordered ceremony and meal that ushered in the week of Passover. (See Maror)

Selah – The Hebrew root of this word is "calah" which means, "to hang." This word denotes a hanging scale used in order to weigh something. The word selah means to weigh what is being said in order to determine or understand its value.

Set Gifts – According to 1 Corinthians 12:28 God set certain gifts within the church. The Greek word for set is tithemi (tith'-ay-mee) which means "to place." The root word of tithemi is histemi (his'-tay-mee) which means "to stand". The set gift or tithemai is the standing placement or the standing order of placement done by the Lord. The set gifts are the five-fold ministry which is apostle, prophet, evangelist, Pastor and teacher and they denote the set order of the Lord as it pertains to His leadership within the Body of Christ.

Seven Spirits of God - Spirit of Lordship, Spirit of Wisdom, Spirit of Knowledge, Spirit of Council, Spirit of Power, Spirit of Obedience, Spirit of Fear or Reverential Awe (Isaiah 11:2; Rev. 3:1)

Shechem (the spirit of) – Shechem raped Dinah who was the daughter of Jacob and Leah. The spirit of Shechem is the spirit of rape, which denotes to violently take something by force without permission. The end thereof is the victim feeling worthless, degrading and lacks confidence. (See rape, Dinahism)

Shewbread – Shewbread was the bread placed in the Sanctuary of the Tabernacle. It was also known as the "Bread of the Presence" or "Bread of the Face." It means the bread laid before God in His presence. Shewbread denotes communion and fellowship with the Father. Each loaf contained about 4 quarts of fine flour. The loaves were pierced (punctured) which speaks of ministers becoming broken in order to serve with the understanding and compassion of Christ. Constant communion and fellowship require constant eating and breaking of bread and wine within the Holy Place, for the bread could only be eaten by the Priests in the Holy Place (the second room). This fact speaks of a union and unity amongst the preachers. The Shewbread was covered by frankincense, which represents an element of praise. On the seventh day the priest would go in and eat the bread. The seventh day represents the Day of God in which we rest in Him. It also pertains to the local ministry resting in the realm of preparation of the vision. Christ is referred to in Scripture as "The Bread of life" (John 6:35), "The Bread that came from heaven" (John 6:33), and "The Living bread" (John 6:51). If we eat of the Bread of Life and drink His blood, then we have eternal life (John 6:54).

Shin - the twenty-first letter of the Hebrew alphabet and is equivalent to the English letters "sh" and "s." The word shin means "tooth". In order to fully understand one must note the act. Teeth are used to grip, to bite to take a hold off and the word shin prophetically speaks of one who grips a hold to something mainly the Word.

Shoe Covenant - The two parties would exchange sandals signifying that the covenant was in effect until the sandals were returned. This was the type of covenant Boaz the kinsman-redeemer made in order to redeem Ruth (Ruth 4:8).

Shofar – a trumpet made of a rams horn. The horn has a crisp clear distinctive sound in which those who are of God are able to hear. Prophetically the shofar is the voice of the Holy Spirit to the Church. The shofar is also the voice of those who are in leadership.

Simeon - Simeon was the second son of Jacob and Leah and father of the tribe of Simeon, one of the twelve tribes of Israel. The Hebrew meaning of his name means "God has heard that I was unloved" (Genesis 29:33). He and his brother Levi destroyed the entire village of Shechem in retribution for the rape of their sister Dinah (Genesis 34).

Simon (the spirit) – In acts chapter 8, Simon was a man who used sorcery to bewitch the people and the people called him "the great power of God." Simon saw the apostles moving in the Holy Ghost and wanted to purchase that power. The spirit of Simon denotes one who uses any means necessary to fool or bewitch the people of God. This is a person who has no desire to seek God or to sacrifice but uses gimmicks in order to convince the people that he or she is some great power of God. It is a false preacher attempting to bewitch God's people. (see Jezebel, soothsayer)

Sin Offering – It is called the chatat in Hebrew (Lev. 4:2). This offering was not a sweet-savor offering. This offering is one that was necessary in order to remove incurred guilt and served to expiate unintentional sins. The burnt offering was all for God; the sin offering was all for man. The word chatat comes from the word chata, which means, "to miss the mark." The verb chet means sin or guilt, also refers to the offering that cancels out sin. The ashes were spread outside the camp showing sins put away. The believer is seen identified with Christ in the burnt offering, however in the sin offering, Christ is seen as identified with the believers sin.

Six Hundred Sixty-Six (666) – The number six hundred and sixty-six denotes the beast and antichrist. Please note that the scripture, which denotes this number, is found in the thirteenth chapter of Revelation. The number thirteen denotes the number for rebellion. There were three men in scripture that were enemies against God and His people. The first being Goliath mentioned in 1 Samuel 17. Goliath's height was 6 cubits, he had 6 pieces of armor and his spear's head weighed 600 shekels of iron. The second of the three men was Nebuchadnezzar whose image, which he set up, was 60 cubits (Dan. 3:1) and the people were to worship his image once they heard the music from six (6) specific instruments. The third man being the Antichrist whose number is 666 as revealed in Revelation 13:8. The number 666 is also the number that denotes the trinity of human perfection; it is the perfection of the imperfection; it is the culmination of human pride in independence of God and opposition to His Christ. The number 666 was the secret symbol of the ancient pagan mysteries connected with the worship of the Devil and today connects ancient mysteries, spiritualism and Theosophy.

Smyrna (the Church) – The second of the seven churches mentioned in Revelation chapter two which was 35 miles north of Ephesus. The message to this church represents a period of great persecution. Smyrna was known for its commerce, wealth and splendor. Its buildings won for the city, the name "The Beautiful." Smyrna was most famous for its "streets of gold" which began with the temple of Zeus and ended with the temple of Cybele who was the goddess of nature. Smyrna is not named in the book of Acts, nor is it named in any of Paul's epistles therefore we have no way of knowing exactly when or how the gospel was introduced to the people in Smyrna. The laws against Christianity were enforced severely in Smyrna. Jews and heathens forced the authorities to carry out their laws against the Christians. The problem with this church was they looked for the prestigious members, they did not require a personal conversation and faith in Jesus Christ. They wanted to grow and be prestigious in the community. Christ said if you overcome, "I'll give you a crown of life." (See Laodicea, Philadelphia, Sardis, Thyatira, Pergamos, Ephesus)

Soothsayer – From the Greek word manteuomai (mant-yoo'-om-ahee) This word is a derivative of the Greek word mainomai which means a craving or longing for, to rave as a maniac. The word manteuomai means a prophet who raves or a raving mad prophet. The spirit of a soothsayer is the spirit of a raving made false prophet.

Sorcery - the practice of magic by some sort of mechanical and manipulative process. It is an attempt to provoke manifestations by using potions and intoxicants that causes an allusion to appear as real and authentic. Sorcery is used with the aid of unclean spirits, it is the practice of witchcraft, magic, spell casting or conjuring. (See witchcraft, divination)

Spirit Filled – a term used amongst those who believe in the Pentecostal experience. It means the indwelling of the Holy Spirit, which then allows you to speak with other tongues as the Spirit gives utterance.

Stewardship – to care for something or someone entrusted to you. Stewardship causes one to keep a thing in mind and to remain focused. It allows you to be consistent in functioning in a particular area. Stewardship requires a thought pattern of principles, which will in turn allow one to handle the possessions that God has entrusted. If God has entrusted you with some-thing, you have dominion over it.

Stipe – The upright piece of the cross. Stipes weighed between 175 and 225 pounds. (See patibulum)

Supernatural – that which operates beyond the norm. The supernatural operates in the realm of the Spirit; it is the means by which the naturally impossible becomes possible.

Synoptic Gospels –the first three books of the New Testament, Matthew Mark and Luke. All three books views are so similar and can be viewed together.

Tabernacle of David – The tent that King David set up on Mount Zion in Jerusalem to house the Ark of the Covenant. David placed certain priests and Levites there as singers and musicians s to minister before the Ark of God daily.

Tabernacle of Moses – The tabernacle was a portable tent that was moved with the Israelites during their wanderings in the wilderness. The tabernacle was also referred to as the tent which consisted of three rooms, the outer court, the Holy Place and the Most Holy Place.

Tav - the last letter of the Hebrew alphabet and is equivalent to the English letter "t" which has retained its cross shape. The Hebrew letter Tav denotes a cross or mark. It is also defined as a sign in the form of a cross used to mark animals. In Ezekiel 9:6 if any man had the sign of a cross on their forehead they were spared from judgment. The letter tav prophetically speaks of our protection it literally denotes the cross at Calvary.

Teth – the ninth letter of the Hebrew alphabet. The Hebrew letter teth's shape resembles that of a serpent. Its meaning is that which is coiled, twisted, rolled. Many lexicons denote teth as to mean a serpent.

Theology – the study of the existence of God

The Lord's Table - also known as communion or celebration of the Eucharist is the observance of what Christ did for His church. It is the celebration of the remembrance of Christ' death.

Thirteen - The number thirteen denotes rebellion. It is found some fifteen times in the Bible; Jesus mentions thirteen things when He gave a picture of the rebellious heart of man (Mark 7:21-22).

Three Anointings – The three Anointings speak of the three offices that were shadowed forth upon King David and fulfilled in Jesus the Messiah. The anointings were:

- David the Prophet – the prophet (Acts 2:29-30)

- David the King – the ministry of reigning and ruling (Ps. 2; 72;110)
- David the Priest – the ministry of the sanctuary, reconciliation (2 Sam. 6:17)

Threshing Floor - a floor or ground area for threshing or treading out grain. David built an altar on Ornan's threshing-floor (2 Sam 24:18-24; 1 Ch 21:18-27), which later became the site of the Temple (2 Ch 3:1). Ruth reveals herself to Boaz on his threshing-floor (Ruth 3:6-9). Prophetically speaking the threshing floor is the place of prayer and during that time of prayer the process of separation, threshing and weeding takes place. It is the place where God gets the leaven out of the believer. (See Moriah, Akedah)

Thyatira (the church) - Thyatira was the fourth of the seven churches mentioned in Revelation chapter two. It was seen as a lax church that was southwest from Pergamos. It has been said that the road from Thyatira to Pergamos is one of the most beautiful in the entire world. Paul's first convert was a woman from Thyatira named Lydia. Lydia was a merchant that dealt in purple linen who became one of Paul's greatest supporters. Of the seven churches, Thyatira is the only church where a women is mentioned by the name of Jezebel. She was the wicked wife of King Ahab and was an idolatress, a murderer and she ran the kingdom. Jezebel is most remembered for her ability to advance idol worship in Israel. The spirit of Jezebel here in of Revelation is a prototype of the Jezebel in the Old Testament. "Her children" is a reference to the offspring's produced from that spirit which was born through Jezebel being allowed to teach and work in the church. The message to Thyatira is the longest of the seven churches. This message presents the hopeless, helpless, corrupt condition of the local church in which it will not emerge, a condition that is absolutely incapable of being improved. There was really no great persecution like the other six churches. Thyatira was almost free from Roman and Greek torture. They knew little about what it meant to suffer for Jesus Christ. Jesus told them in Thyatira that have not partaken of the doctrine of Jezebel that he would put no other burden upon them. He encourages them to hold fast until He comes. He promises to those that overcome he will give power over nations and shall rule with him a rod of iron. (See Laodicea, Philadelphia, Sardis, Smyrna, Pergamos, Ephesus)

Time

- Aion (ahee-ohn') – period or age for God's purpose and timing.
- Season – mo'ed, which means "appointed time."
- Chronos (khron'-os) – time allotted in order to do the will of God
- Kairos (kahee-ros') – space or time for opportunity or special occasion.
- Chronotribeo (khron-ot-rib-eh'-o) Wasted time, a procrastinator, a lingerer.
- Proskairos (pros'-kahee-ros;) – Temporary season. The enemy will attack for a proskairos however the Lord will deliver the believer. Every believer will go through their temporary season of attack but the Lord delivers us out of them all!

Titilus – a placard that indicated the crime of an individual being crucified. In Jesus' case His Titilus read "Jesus king of the Jews." This indicated that Christ was being crucified for setting Himself up as a king in rebellion against Tiberius Caesar. (See Stipe, patibulum)

Traditions – on going functions passed down from one generation to another. That which is passed down contains no type of alteration.

Trespass Offering – It is called Asham in the Hebrew (Lev. 5:14). This also is known as the guilt offering or penalty offering. There are three types of sins represented in this particular offering and all are unpremeditated which required a sin offering: (1) withholding evidence when called upon to testify: the voice of swearing (a summons to testify) (2) a case of accidental ceremonial defilement by contact with an unclean animal or man (3) being unable to fulfill a rash vow. All three were considered unpremeditated sins however there was still the requiring of the offering. The trespass offering, another nonsweet-savor offering, was a sacrifice for the sins of nature. The sin offering dealt with the root of sin while the trespass offering dealt with the fruit of sin. The trespass offering was of expiation, the guilt of sin was taken away it was also of restoration; that which was lost by the first Adam is restored by the second Adam the Lord Jesus. It also involved restitution; the offerer was to restore to the person that which he had unjustly taken, and he was to add a fifth part to it to compensate for the wrong. The Trespass

Offering represents a settling of two parties. It also settled ill feelings between two parties that were in disagreement. Christ settled the disagreement between God and man.

Trumpets (Feast of) – The Feast of Trumpets is a festival that happens in the fall and is observed on the first day of the seventh month at a new moon or a change of season. The Jews call this day Rosh Hashanah, which is the New Year, so the feast of trumpets began the New Year. The feast of Trumpets serves as an introduction to the Feast of Tabernacles (Ingathering). The trumpet referred to here was the shofar (a ram's horn). The shofar from a Spiritual standpoint represents an utterance coming from the Lord, a prophetic word from the Lord. The Feast of the Trumpets represents a season of prophetic utterance, a word from God. (See Passover, unleavened bread, firstfruits, Pentecost, day of the trumpet, Day of Atonement, feast of Tabernacles)

Trust – There are three Hebrew words that assist in understanding the word for trust. The first word is the Hebrew word chakah (khaw-saw') which gives the idea of one fleeing for protection or running to a shelter. If one trusts in something then they can run to it. Another word for trust is betahh, which means "to cling as to cling to a vine." The third word for trust is yachal (yaw-chal') which means "to hope." To hope means to know or have confidence in. The three words listed give a clear understanding of trust. Trust means to flee to someone for protection, to cling to protection and to hope as to know or have confidence in. (See faith)

Truth – Truth is the living vital powerful demonstration of the Spirit of God pulsating with divine life, power, wisdom and knowledge.

Twelve - The number twelve denotes divine government, apostolic fullness and order. There were twelve tribes of Israel this speaks of church government. Twelve stones in the high priest breastplate that signifies that the priest is to govern the spiritual order of the church.

Twelve Tribes - the twelve sons of Jacob who were the ancestors of Israel. Each occupied a separate territory (except the tribe of Levi, which was set apart to serve in the Holy Temple). The tribes were the nation of God which served as a type of spiritual family of God. The twelve tribes were Asher, Benjamin, Dan, Gad, Issachar, Joseph (Manasseh, Ephraim were the sons of

Joseph adopted by Jacob and were part of the tribe of Simeon and Reuben), Judah, Levi, Naphtali, Reuben, Simeon, Zebulun.

Tzaddi - the eighteenth letter of the Hebrew alphabet that denotes a fishhook. Tzaddi prophetically speaks of the church being the fishhook catching fish for the kingdom by using the bait of the Gospel.

Unction – the anointing that enables a believer to do kingdom work. It causes the individual to function beyond the norm operating in the supernatural. The anointing destroys the yoke and without the unction (anointing) nothing will be accomplished. (See anointing)

Unicity – It is the quality or state of being unique of its kind.

Unity – It is the singleness of mind that pursues God's purpose

Unleavened Bread (The Feast of) – is closely associated with the Passover because the Israelites ate the roasted lamb and unleavened bread that night in Egypt. The blood is the foundation of fellowship with God; the eating of the lamb and bread represents maintaining that fellowship. As we continually eat the Unleavened Bread and are restored, we will preach a message of restoration. The Day of Unleavened Bread speaks of Christ, our Restoration. The unleavened bread prophetically denotes an uncompromised word. (see passover, firstfruits)

Uriah – he was the husband of Bathsheba. David seduced the Bathsheba and in doing so impregnated her. Uriah was brought home from the war but refused to sleep with Bathsheba because he felt he should have been on the battle field with his brothers. David then had Uriah placed in the heat of the battle where he was killed. God judged David for his action. Uriah denotes a believer who loves God and loves to operate in warfare regardless of the cost. This type of believer is one of great integrity.

Urim and Thummim – A pouch in the breastplate that sat directly over the heart housed the Urim and the Thummim. The priest used the Urim and Thummim to receive direction from the Lord. The word Urim means "light" while the word Thummim means "completeness or perfection." The two words Urim and Thummim translated mean "lights, perfection or revelational truth" better known as "revelation knowledge." The revelation of Christ is constantly revealed in the mind of the pastor. The Urim and Thummim in the pouch of the breastplate represents the spirit of revelation. The spirit of revelation is used to receive direction from the Lord as it pertains to the direction of the ministry.

Usury – an amount of money paid for the use of money meaning interest. The interest was to be very excessive. Jews were forbidden to exploit usury amongst each other and violation of that law was considered a great crime. The believer does not operate in the spirit of usury and such an operation is in violation of the law of God. (Lev. 25:36, 37)

Uz (The Land of) – the place where Job lived. It was his place of testing and transition. (Job 1:1)

Uzzah – the son of Abinadab who along with his brother Ahio was transporting the Ark back from the Philistines into Jerusalem. While transporting the Ark, the ox-cart stumbled causing Uzzah to reach his hand out to steady the Ark. Touching the Ark was in direct violation of divine law in Numbers 4:15. Uzzah was immediately smitten to death. Uzzah teaches to know the ways of God before attempting to handle the articles and ministries of God.

Uzziah – He was a descendant of Levi and a father to one of David's treasurers (1 Chron. 27:25). He was also known as Azariah and was son and successor of King Amaziah of Judah. Uzziah was declared king by the people of Judah when he was sixteen and reigned for 52 years which was the second longest reign of a king in the history of Judah. King Uzziah at one time was a king who honored God but eventually moved out of the will of God and did something that he was not supposed to do. He went into the priests' office and attempted to offer up incense. The priests in the temple attempted to stop him but were unsuccessful. His disobedience caused him to end up with leprosy and his disobedience also caused Judah to be devastated according to Zechariah 14:4-5.

Vain - actions or words that are void of function or purpose causing failure or disappointment.

Vav - this sixth letter of the Hebrew alphabet that denotes a hook or a nail, some type of fastener or connecter.

Veil – The veil in the Old Testament was the Hebrew word poreketh, which means "a sacred screen." The New Testament word for veil is katapetasma, which means, "Something spread thoroughly." The veil was a four-inch screen-like curtain that spread thoroughly before the Most Holy Place. It was 17-½ feet high and four inches think; it took 60 men to handle the veil. It was made of fine linen interwoven with the colors blue, purple and scarlet. The veil was also embroidered with figures of cherubims. It was to be hung on four pillars made of shittim wood overlaid with gold. Josephus reported that the veil was four inches think and was renewed each year and that horses tied to each side of the veil could not pull the veil apart. The veil barred all but the High Priest from the Presence of the Lord. The veil covers the unmanifested promises. The veil causes one to remember, honor, and respect the sacredness of God; it also admonishes those to not take the works of Christ and His divine order for granted. The veil represents a passing through and ascending to the third dimension; it is a moving from one glory to another.

Virgin – Mary the mother of Jesus was a virgin who brought forth a son. The body of Christ is a virgin who is to bring forth the child Jesus the Christ. As the Holy Spirit came upon Mary, so does the Holy Spirit come upon the Church of God causing it to produce a Son.

Vision - the will of God revealed which would cause an individual to impact planet earth for the kingdom of God.

Voice – the Hebrew word qowl (kole) found in Psalms 29:4. This word denotes a shepherd who is able to call the sheep and they will swiftly come. This voice is the voice the Father has given to His leaders, as they speak those who hear come or come up to what God is saying. A voice serves as a leader that opens the door or way of opportunity either in a positive or negative way. A negative voice will have as much impact on a generation as a positive voice will because a voice either positive or negative will bring some type of change. There was a voice that walked in the Garden in the cool of the day. The voice of the blood of Abel cried out unto the Lord from the ground. Yes a voice can bring change, but in this writing we are going to focus on the voice of the Church.

Vow – a voluntary promise expected to be kept if the vow was made with the right intensions.

Warfare – The Old Testament word for warfare is tsaba' (tsaw-baw') which means a mass of persons organized for war. One of the New Testament word for warfare is strateuomai (strat-yoo'-om-ahee) which means, "to serve in a military campaign," "to execute the apostolate with its arduous duties and functions, to contend inclinations." Warfare is the military position of one in leadership and the position of that leader is to execute the apostolate. The job of the apostle is to war against anything that opposes truth and revelation.

Wave –Heave Offering – The breast and thigh of each peace offering are to be given to the priest (Lev. 7:30-32). In a wave offering the breast of the animal was waved back and forth toward and away from the altar as a symbol of presenting the offering to God and of His returning it to the priest. The wave offering is known as a tenufah, which according to rabbinic sources is "a waving." The worshiper was to stand before the altar holding the portions in his hands and the priest was to move the hands of the sacrificer back and forth horizontally and then up and down. The heave offering is known as the terumah. It consisted of heaving the right shoulder of the animal up and down symbolically setting it aside as a contribution to God for the use of His priest. In order for God to accept any offering, it had to first be placed on the altar at the tent of the tabernacle. The altar means the place of sacrifice. The cross is the New Testament place of sacrifice so the Old Testament altar refers to the New Testament cross. Remember that Old Testament foundations establish New Testament truths. It is at the altar that we remain dead, but alive in God. It is at the cross that we remain free, humble, and we keep seeing the light and purpose of God.

Wilderness – The English dictionary describes wilderness as a place for the wildlife, land that is uninhabited. What lives in the wilderness? Animals live in the wilderness and it is there that they learn how to function and survive. The Hebrew word for wilderness is midbar (mid-bawr') which means "an open field, a pasture." The root word for wilderness is the Hebrew word dabar (daw-bar') that means "an arrangement or order." The wilderness is a place of learning, it is in this area that one is taught and learns how to survive. The wilderness is the place where one learns how to become organized for the purpose of the Kingdom. The Children of Israel came out of Egypt and into the wilderness before they could go into the Promised Land.

Will (The) – What one wishes or has determined shall be done. The will of God for ones life is that which the Father has already determined shall be done

Wineskins – Wineskin were used for carrying fluids. They were made by killing an animal and cutting off its head and feet. The carcass was skinned and all of the holes except the neck were sewn together. New wine that was poured into these skins would still be fermenting so the skin had to be moist and young enough to handle the build up of fermenting gas. If the skin was young enough the new wine would not split the skin. If the skin was old and brittle, then the fermenting wine would split the skin causing the new wine to leak out. New wine was placed in new wineskins that were pliable and elastic enough to accommodate the pressure. Prophetically speaking, if one is going to house the new wine of God, then the house needs to be moist or revived enough so that when the new wine shifts, inside of the skin, the skin will be able to move with the shifting of the wine. If there is going to be a new wine, then there will have to be a new wineskin (bottle) to house the new wine. The new wine cannot be mixed with anything old.

Witchcraft – the practice of divination, or sorcery. The devils agents operate in witchcraft in order to produce the devils' will. (See divination, sorcery)

Works of the flesh - Operations of the flesh which if allowed to function can become destructive to the local assembly and to the body of Christ. The works of the flesh are noted in Galatians 5: 19-21 and they are adultery, fornication, uncleanness, lasciviousness, idolatry, witchcraft, hatred, variance, emulations, wrath, strife, seditions, heresies, envyings, murders, drunkenness, and revellings. Such works of the flesh will not inherit the kingdom of God.

Writings (The) – the third division of the Old Testament Hebrew Bible which consisted of eleven books were divided into three books of poetry-Psalms, Proverbs, and Job; five rolls or scrolls (Megilloth) The Song of Solomon, Ruth, Lamentations, Ecclesiastes, and Esther; one book of prophecy-Daniel; two books of history-Ezra-Nehemiah and Chronicles.

Xenodocheo – The Greek word which means to receive or entertain strangers and to show hospitality. (1 Tim 5:10).

Xeraino – xeraino (xay-rah'ee-no) the Greek word for withered. This word denotes something that becomes shriveled or dries up. This withering speaks of a believer who has not much root in the Word. When the enemy comes will cause you to xeraino because of no root.

Yad – an ornament usually made of silver used as a pointer. When a person was called upon to read from the Torah a pointer or yad was used. The scrolls were made of parchment and were considered extremely sacred so touching the scroll with the natural hand was forbidden. In the Hebrew the word yad is translated "hand" and it was intended to prevent anyone from touching the parchment with their hands.

Yahweh – According to Jewish tradition the name Yahweh was forbidden to pronounce except by the High Priest in the Holy of Holies on Yom Kippur (Day of Atonement). There has been debate of the name Yahweh and as for its origin it is uncertain. Yahweh today is known as the name of the God of Israel, as preserved in the original consonantal Hebrew Bible text. The Tetragrammaton (the first four consonants of the word Yahweh (YHWH) is more commonly used as it is consistent with the Hebrew letters used for the name of God.

Yod - is the smallest letter of the Hebrew alphabet. In Matthew 5:18, Jesus referred to the Hebrew alphabet when He said not one jot (yod) or tittle shall in any wise pass from the law until all be fulfilled. Jewish writers interpret the yod or hand as denoting power and possession. Yod is defined as the "open hand." The open hand indicates power, strength and blessing.

Yoke – this word speaks of a type of bondage. Yoke also means to join together by coupling at the neck with another in order to assure submission, steady direction and work. Jesus said Matthew 11:29-30 "take my yoke upon you and learn of me." The believer is to get connected by the neck in order to learn the submission, steady direction and work of the kingdom.

Yom Kippur – see Atonement Day of

Zadok - joined David at Hebron, he accompanied David when he fled from Jerusalem, He was appointed by David to anoint Solomon to be king. Zadok was a high priest that was faithful to David and Solomon his leaders he understood commitment.

Zayin – the seventh letter of the Hebrew alphabet which means "a weapon." It is shaped like a dagger or a sword. Prophetically speaking zayin is the seventh letter, seven speaks of that which is complete; zayin is shaped like a sword or a dagger which denotes the word, it also denotes the weapon of the kingdom which is the Word of God.

Zeal – From the Greek word zelos (dzay'-los) which means "hot." This word could be used in a good sense or a bad sense. In a good sense it speaks of one having zeal meaning passion for the things of God. In a bad or negative sense the word zeal denotes a spirit of jealousy.

Zealots – a name applied to Jews who where devoted to defending the honor of God and Israel. The Hebrew term is Kannaim, which means "one who is jealous on behalf of God." It is from this word zealots that the English word zeal comes from. (See zeal)

Zebulun – the sixth son of Jacob and Leah. The tribe of Zebulun is noted in the special praise of Deborah the judge. During the battle against Sisera Zebulun fought valiantly alongside the tribe of Naphtali. Zebulun prophetically speaks of warfare and order, when one is able to fight the enemy and stand their ground it will bring defeat.

Zechariah – His name means Jehovah is renowned or remembered. He was a seeing prophet and experienced many visions. In Zechariah 1 through 6:8 he has eight visions in one night that dealt with the history of Israel. He was contemporary with Haggai and was responsible for speaking an encouraging word to Zerubbabel to lay the foundation for the temple.

Zephaniah – was a prophet during the reign of Josiah known for prophesying to the people concerning idol worship and for their practice of foreign customs.

Zerubbabel – A Leader of the Jews. Tradition states that he also acted as governor of Judah. He returned from Babylonian exile and was encouraged by the prophets Zechariah and Haggai to rebuild the temple at Jerusalem.

Zidonians (The) – the Zidonians were the inhabitants of Zidon who at one time oppressed Israel. They were skillful in hewing timber and eventually were employed by both David and Solomon to hew cedar trees. They worshiped the god Ashtoreth which is who Solomon built temples for so that his wives could worship that same god.

Zion – originally the name of one of the hills in Jerusalem. Zion subsequently became the term for the Holy City. It was eventually destroyed because of Israel's disobedience. Today Zion is being restored and will once again be noted for its singing, rejoicing, righteous judgments, safety and prophecy.

References and Works Cited

The Theological Wordbook. Nashville: Word Publishing, 2003

Robinson, Robert. **The Ministry of the Tabernacle**. Kearney: Morris Publishing. 1999

Robinson, Robert. **The Numbers "God's Numbers Revealed."** Cranston: Davedez Publishing. 2006

Robinson, Robert. **Revelation The Book**. Cranston: Davedez Publishing 1995

About the Author

Dr. Robert Robinson is a speaker and teacher of church government and spiritual order as it pertains to a last day outpouring of God's anointing. In 1986, he entered the ministry and is presently the Senior Pastor of The House of Manna Ministries in Cranston, RI and is also the presiding prelate of the Rhema Covenant Fellowship. Dr. Robinson has authored over twenty-five books. Apostle Robinson is a Father and Pastor to many Pastors. He is married to his wife Glenda and both have been blessed with two children, David and Desere'. Dr. Robinson has traveled extensively throughout the United States in the ministry gift of an apostle, prophet, and teacher in churches, conventions, and seminars and continues to do so.

For information on other material by Dr. Robert Robinson Please contact

Dr. Robert L Robinson Ministries
PO Box 10106
Cranston, RI 02910
(401) 228-6108
Houseofmannaministries.com
Drrobinsonministries.com

Other Titles
by Dr. Robert Robinson

An Appointed Time
An encouragement to those who have been sidelined by the works of the enemy.

A Sevenfold Purpose
The Sevenfold Purpose is the revealing of the will of God to His church as it pertains to alignment and order.

A survey of the Old Testament
This book gives information pertaining to the Old Testament. A survey of the Old Testament deals with the History of Israel, their Kings, prophets, priests and ordinances.

A survey of the Old Testament Workbook
The workbook to A survey of the Old Testament

A Time To Work
This book serves as a word to believers concerning a period when God will release an anointing for seed and harvest

Build Me A House
A motivational prophetic Word based on the book of Ezra.

Build Me A House Correspondence Course
Correspondence Course based on the book entitled "Build Me A House."

Can These Bones Live?
A writing based on the book of Ezekiel 37:1-14.

Hebrews Chapter Nine "The Interpretation"
This book is a verse by verse commentary on the ninth chapter of the book of Hebrews.

His Praise
This book teaches of the Hebrew Praise Words.

How we got the Bible
This book gives information concerning the history and makeup of the Bible. It deals with the many testing that were done in order to prove its authenticity.

How we got the Bible Workbook
This is the workbook to the book entitled "How we got the Bible." In it you will find questions that will assist you in developing an understanding for the history of the Bible.

Lessons I've Learned
This book is a compilation of bible studies taught by Dr. Robinson.

Revelation The Book
A commentary of the New Testament prophetical book of Revelations.

Revelation The Book Workbook
This is the workbook to "Revelation the Book."

The Authority of the Kingdom
This writing serves as a wakeup call to all believers in regards to what the Father has invested in the kingdom Due out November 2007

The Ministry of the Tabernacle
This book is gives detailed information on the Tabernacle of Moses. This book includes the work book

The Ministry of the Tabernacle Workbook
The Workbook to the book The Ministry of the Tabernacle.

The Necessity For Leadership
This book deals with the need and importance of spiritual leadership.

The Numbers
The Numbers serves as a book of explanation of numbers throughout the Scripture.

Made in the USA
Lexington, KY
09 January 2010